St. Louis Community College

FOREST PARK LIBRARY

Library

5801 Wilson Avenue
St. Louis, Missouri 63110

PSYCHOLOGICAL
ASPECTS OF
NUCLEAR WAR

James Thompson

*Adopted as a Statement by the Council of
The British Psychological Society
at its meeting on 13 October 1984.*

Published by the British Psychological Society
and John Wiley & Sons Limited.
Chichester New York Brisbane Toronto Singapore

© The British Psychological Society, 1985
First edition
ISBN 0 471 90747 2

 British Library Cataloguing in Publication Data

Thompson, James A.
  Psychological aspects of nuclear war.
  1. Nuclear warfare——Psychological aspects
  I. Title   II. British Psychological Society
  355'.0127   U263

Published by The British Psychological Society
and John Wiley & Sons Limited

Distributed by John Wiley & Sons Limited
Chichester New York Brisbane Toronto Singapore

Members of the British Psychological Society
should order the book direct from
St. Andrews House,
48 Princess Road East,
Leicester, LE1 7DR, UK.

Typeset by Communitype, Wigston, Leicester
Printed and bound in Great Britain by AB Printers Limited, Leicester

Foreword

At an Open Meeting during The British Psychological Society's Annual Conference on 10 April 1983, it was proposed that a statement should be issued by the Society on the contribution of psychology to the nuclear debate. The proposed statement was to be limited to certain areas of this large issue and was intended as an objective review of evidence.

This proposal was considered by the Council of the British Psychological Society on 21 May 1983. The decision was taken to invite Dr James Thompson, in consultation with other psychologists, to prepare a statement concentrating on 'the psychological assumptions behind current civil defence planning and the likely psychological state of those who survive the immediate effects of nuclear bombing; human fallibility and the risk of accidental nuclear explosion; and conflict and negotiations'. It is, of course, to be considered in conjunction with other statements based on medical knowledge, on physical and metereological information, and on political or military theory.

Because the Council were concerned that the statement should be a scholarly, non-partisan review of the relevant literature, it was decided to go through a rigorous refereeing process, as is usual with scientific papers published in the Society's journals. Dr Chris Leach, Chairperson of the Society's Journals Committee and an experienced Editor of one of the Society's Journals, was asked to act as Editor for the statement. The first draft was sent to seven anonymous referees, all eminent British psychologists, chosen for their expertise in the various substantive areas reviewed in the text. Their suggestions contributed to the final version, which was seen by two of the original referees. As a result, the statement has been subjected to more thorough scrutiny than is customary even with the careful anonymous peer refereeing procedures for the Society's journals.

The statement is not about the immorality of war, nuclear or otherwise, nor is it about the current politics of disarmament. Rather, it provides readers with a fuller information base on which to formulate their opinions on the issue of nuclear war, and indicates the ways in which psychological knowledge might usefully be applied in this area.

We, the undersigned, were successively Presidents of the British Psychological Society when the Statement on psychological aspects of nuclear war was planned in April 1983 and published in March 1985. The book has the status of a Statement adopted by the Council of the Society on these important issues.

Professor Ian Howarth, President, BPS, 1984-5

Dr Halla Beloff, Vice-President, BPS, 1984-5; President, BPS, 1983-4

January 1985

Page CONTENTS

ACKNOWLEDGEMENTS

My task has been to be editor as much as author, and very many people have contributed material, references, thoughts and advice. The choice of what to include has been my own responsibility.

The scientific background to the physical devastation of nuclear war was provided by Phil Steadman and Owen Greene at the Open University, and I made extensive use of their writings on this subject. Vladimir Alexandrov at the Computing Centre of the USSR Academy of Sciences gave me additional findings on the modelling of the climatic consequences of nuclear war.

The original material on civil defence was provided by John Churcher and Elena Lieven at Manchester University, and I am also indebted to them for much of the work on psychological consequences of disasters. Professor Rachel Rosser kindly discussed disaster reactions with me, and suggested material I should look at which had appeared since her original review.

Data on human fallibility came from a research group in which Chris Cull and Aleda Erskine played a major part. Margaret Ballard provided additional data on drug abuse in military personnel. The staff at the Institute for the Study of Drug Disorders were very helpful in gathering relevant material.

Professor David Canter at Guildford University provided me with material on design aspects of accident prevention.

A perspective on negotiation and conflict resolution, together with much helpful material, was provided by Dr Oppenheim at the London School of Economics.

Particular thanks are due to Herb Blumberg, who provided many photocopies of papers, assisted with literature searches, and commented on early drafts of some of the first sections. Herbert Abrams at Harvard Medical School guided me to new material in the field of accidents, and Milton Leitenberg at The Swedish Institute of International Affairs supplied countless papers and references on arms control, as well as commenting on the first draft of the section on accidents.

Bill Ury discussed both the theory and practice of nuclear negotiations with me, and his work made a major contribution to the section on conflict resolution.

As part of the Council's assessment process, five anonymous professors, all Fellows of The British Psychological Society, commented on the first draft of the statement. All provided helpful advice, additional references and in several cases detailed critical comment. This refereeing process has considerably improved the document, although it was not possible to incorporate every suggestion in the final draft. I am grateful to all of them for their help.

Chris Leach cast an experienced editorial eye over both the first draft and the five professorial assessments. Together we were able to find a way of using these comments to produce the second draft, and I am very grateful for all his work.

Margaret Ballard read and commented on all sections of the statement, and assisted me at every stage of its production. She also had to put up with many empty evenings, so I owe her a double debt of gratitude.

My particular thanks to Joyce Collins and Christopher Feeney for all the editorial and indexing work done under considerable time pressure.

All those who kindly helped me are listed below.

Dr Herbert Abrams
Dr Vladimir Alexandrov
Ms Margaret Ballard
Dr R. Benjamin
Dr Michael Berger
Dr H.P. Blumberg
Mr Stuart Britten
Professor David Canter
Dr David Childs
Dr Eric Chivian
Mr John Churcher
Professor W.P. Colquhoun
Ms Chris Cull
Dr Malcolm Dando
Professor Lloyd Dumas
Professor J. Richard Eiser
Ms Aleda Erskine
Dr Chris French
Dr Owen Green
Professor Robert Green

Dr James Hemmings
Dr Nick Humphrey
Dr Chris Leach
Dr Milton Leitenberg
Dr Elena Lieven
Professor Robert Jay Lifton
Dr Stuart Linke
Dr. C.R. Mitchell
Professor T. Moore
Professor John Morton
Dr A.N. Oppenheim
Professor Mike Penz
Dr Gwyn Prins
Professor Rachel Rosser
Dr J. Rowan
Dr Philip Steadman
Professor G. Stephenson
Professor Barbara Tizard
Dr Marian Tysoe
Dr William Ury
Dr Valerie Yule

SUMMARY

There are three main themes to the statement. The first is the way people are likely to react in the event of nuclear war. There is a lack of direct evidence in this area so extrapolations are made from research that has been carried out into other kinds of disaster. The implications for civil defence preparations are then discussed. The second theme is the possibility of accidental nuclear explosion. The discussion is based on evidence of human fallibility that has emerged from the psychology of accidents and from research into decision-making in military and political contexts. The third theme draws on the psychology of negotiation and conflict resolution to suggest ways in which the threat of nuclear war might be reduced.

Psychological reactions in the event of nuclear war

It is difficult for us to comprehend either the physical or the psychological effects of a nuclear attack. The limitations of our psychological frameworks and our lack of experience of large-scale disasters combine to give any attempt to conceptualize such an event a measure of unreality. The greater the intensity of the attack, the more difficult it becomes to understand. Careful consideration of such evidence as is available does, however, allow extrapolations to be made.

To start with it is clear that people's estimation of the likelihood of nuclear war is greater than is often assumed. Recent studies have shown that 35–50% of people think such a war to be likely and the level of such anxiety is increasing, particularly amongst the young. The most consistent reaction, however, is some form of 'denial', a failure to acknowledge something that constitutes a psychological (or actual) threat. Such a reaction is akin to the necessary assumption of personal invulnerability that enables us to keep functioning in times of extreme danger.

This denial will still characterize the reactions of a proportion of people as the first warnings are given. Others will make preparations. As warnings intensify and become more accepted as official, anxiety will increase. The effect of this increased anxiety on behaviour will vary. To some extent it will depend upon the amount and quality of information about what people should be doing. The less the information and the more ambiguous it is, the more will behaviour depend on that of others. Many people, particularly the young, will try to move away from urban areas to those areas thought less likely to be affected. Family ties will tend to predominate, with moves for families to get together. Family influences will also operate for designated survival personnel causing those with closer ties to override their official responsibilities. Attempts to restrict movement, or other constraints, will tend to increase anxiety further and strengthen reactions.

Once an explosion has occurred, the general reaction, contrary to common belief, is unlikely to be one of great panic. After an initial period of elation at having survived, the disaster syndrome will tend to predominate. Disaster victims become apathetic, docile, indecisive, unemotional and behave mechanically. Even those who escape physical damage will be subject to pyschological disturbances, in many cases of a severe nature.

The level of psychological distress amongst survivors will increase with the intensity of any attack. So will the length of time before most people will have recovered sufficiently to return to quasi-normal functioning. For some the effects will be permanent and for most of these the degree of impairment will be severe. The conventional resources for helping people cope with such psychological distress will be unlikely to be able to deal with all in need, even in the event of just a single nuclear explosion on an urban centre. However, in such a case, resources from areas not affected will be available to help the gradual return towards normality. With more intense attacks, as more of the country is involved, the chances of a return to normality recede. The level of psychological impairment will be such that the social function-ing necessary to community life will be impossible for many survivors.

Human fallibility

Whenever there is a human element to any system, there is a risk of fallibility. Though safeguards can be built into sophisticated systems, they tend to be designed on the basis of rationality and on the assumption that human performance can be maintained at high levels of skill. Psychological evidence suggests, however, that under conditions of stress and with enhanced time pressure, the ability to make rational decisions deteriorates. No-one is free from these influences.

Research into accidents has highlighted a number of factors that have led to the impairment of skilled performance. Environmental conditions, such as noise, illumination, temperature and the degree of stimulation (both social and perceptual) can directly affect human cognitive processes. These factors can also have indirect effects by influencing the individual's mood. Subjective states can also be temporarily affected by the ingestion of psychoactive drugs and alcohol, which also directly affect task performance. Even tried and tested systems have failed because people have made small errors that have caused emotional states in the operator that then make the probability of other errors higher.

Many of the factors that affect performance are to be found in nuclear weapon control centres. As reliance on automated equipment increases and control systems become more complex, the amount of information that has to be processed can overload the operator so that functioning is impaired. Research in ergonomics has much to offer those responsible for the design of such control systems. Psychology can also help in the screening of personnel, particularly military, for work in nuclear areas.

Although safety measures are improving and can further be improved to prevent accidental explosion, human fallibility could still lead to unplanned nuclear attack. Stress and heightened time pressure not only affect individual skilled performance but also impair rational functioning in decision-making groups, for example, a 'war cabinet'. The psychology of group processes helps us to understand the way in which rigid and polarized positions can be maintained, misperceptions of others can be reinforced, and valid information can be ignored or distorted. In periods of heightened tension, inappropriate reactions to ambiguous events may dangerously worsen the crisis.

These factors, taken together with the shorter decision times imposed by modern weapons systems, signify that crisis decision-making in a nuclear age is inevitably highly risky.

Negotiations and conflict resolution

Our understanding of psychological processes can point the way to possible avenues for productive negotiations. For there to be effective negotiation, there must be effective communication. There must also be a recognition that emotions will play a part. These emotions should be given legitimate means of expression (in the other as well as the self) if they are not to determine the course of the negotiation. In this way a better understanding of the perceptions of other parties can be gained.

There are psychological processes that result in the setting up and maintenance of entrenched positions in negotiations. These processes form barriers to a successful conclusion. Workers in the field have discovered techniques for moving participants away from such positions. These techniques are designed to separate the individuals from the problem and to place a focus on the underlying interests of participants rather than their ostensive positions. By ensuring that all parties are working together on some aspect of the problem, the solution to which can benefit all sides, it is possible to bring about considerable change in attitudes. If the negotiators can be persuaded to spend time in developing a variety of possible options of benefit to both sides and in agreeing on objective criteria for acceptable solutions then the process of negotiation will be smoothed and success be far more likely.

Once we have recognized that psychological factors are intensified as stress and time pressures increase, we can see the importance of putting effort into the prevention of crises. Entrenched positions and distorted perceptions can be reduced if politicians can be persuaded away from emotional rhetoric against the other side which reduces room for manoeuvre. If more of the debate were carried out in private, responses to proposals would be easier. Far better would be to attempt in private to agree a joint proposal which can then be made public.

Increasing personal contact and improving communications could greatly assist the process of negotiation. Problem-solving workshops, which involve middle-ranking military and civilian officers of the superpowers, could go some way towards this. So could the establishment of a crisis control centre, jointly manned by a small group of defence and diplomatic experts from each side. Such a centre could work to devise possible crisis prevention and control measures and facilitate the exchange and validation of information should crises develop.

There are a number of possible common tasks on which the superpowers could become jointly engaged. For example, work could be done on joint procedures for crisis consultation, on accident prevention, and on ways of giving time to decide what to do in a crisis. The superpowers could work on such topics without the emotion that accompanies attempts to negotiate weapon reductions. Joint action in support of mediation efforts in conflicts elsewhere, might also provide a common objective as well as help reduce the possibility of increased tension between the superpowers.

A variety of psychological techniques already exist to enable the process of increasing cooperation rather than continuing competition; to ensure that the motivation to achieve a solution replaces the motivation to seek maximum advantage. Far more use could be made of these techniques than is apparent from current disarmament negotiations.

1

THE NATURE OF THE THREAT

Whether science – and indeed civilization in general – can long survive depends upon psychology, that is to say, it depends upon what human beings desire. Russell (1950)

In order to assess the psychological effects of threatened or actual nuclear war the possible physical effects of such a disaster must be considered. It is difficult to describe the nature of this threat, since the full extent of the massive technological changes in warfare are hard to grasp. Although, in the past, all cultures have had to cope with natural catastrophes and epidemics, none has ever had to cope with the prospect of such widespread sudden destruction.

The power of nuclear explosions cannot readily be understood, since there is nothing in our everyday experience with which to compare them. While the effects of a few pounds of explosives in a terrorist bomb can be comprehended by witnessing the injuries and damage caused, the effects of a million tons of TNT equivalent cannot be understood. Every attempt to describe the extent of the destruction using familiar landmarks gives only partial assistance to our understanding. Our everyday psychological framework is based on the assumption that the physical landscape changes only slowly, and most of our struggles teach us that solid objects in the world remain roughly where they are put unless we exert ourselves to move them. It takes a hurricane or an earthquake to question these assumptions, and such experiences are rare. Any attempt to conceptualize nuclear war comes up against this limitation, and all discussion on the issue has an unreal quality, since we cannot fully believe the self-created threat of nuclear destruction. From the psychological point of view the events to be discussed seem as improbable as our own death.

The nature of the evidence

Nuclear war itself cannot be studied by the traditional scientific procedures of observation, experimentation and replication, and it is to be hoped that there will never be any opportunity to carry out such research.

Findings on the effects of large scale nuclear war will always contain elements of uncertainty, and estimates must be made by drawing careful conclusions from the best available evidence. Such evidence will necessarily be stronger in some areas than others. For example, the physical characteristics of nuclear explosions have been extensively studied in over 1375 detonations since 1945 (SIPRI, 1983), their effects on the atmosphere when used in large numbers over inhabited areas is still thankfully less well known (Turco *et al.*, 1983), and their effects on humans only haphazardly observed in two instances.

Although there have been many accidents involving nuclear weapons, the severity of these cannot easily be estimated when many details are kept secret, nor can the likelihood of future accidents be determined absolutely. Yet the extensive literature on accidents in other fields of human endeavour has a profound bearing on the nuclear case, and this evidence cannot safely be ignored.

Even the data on the number of weapons and their destructive potential can be a source of dispute, and independent sources have been used wherever possible. The research background to the better known publications has been investigated and documented by Albrecht *et al.* (1978), and in general the Stockholm International Peace Research Institute yearbooks have been used for weapons totals because of their better documentation and independent funding.

In order to discuss nuclear matters at all, evidence from many sources must be collated and evaluated. Where there are limitations to the findings and doubts about the evidence, these will be indicated. It is to be hoped that any discussion about nuclear war will always lack any final validation.

Physical effects of nuclear weapons

Many accounts have been given of the physical effects of nuclear explosions (Glasstone and Dolan, 1980; Office of Technology Assessment, 1980; Openshaw, Steadman and Greene, 1983) and the general characteristics are known, though many important effects such as low-level radiation hazards to human subjects (Lindop and Rotblat, 1982), and major atmospheric and climatic changes (Crutzen and Birks, 1983; Turco *et al.*, 1983), remain imprecise.

The main consequence of nuclear detonation is a massive blast wave of such enormous force that it totally destroys everything round it. A flash of light and heat burns everything over a wide area, and depending on whether the bomb bursts near the ground, varying amounts of radioactive fallout are distributed over an even wider area.

Using a bomb of the equivalent of a million tons of TNT as a yardstick, one could expect that if this were detonated at 6000 feet then all buildings within a radius of 2.5 miles would be destroyed and damage of lesser magnitude would be experienced 10 miles away. In all, 101 square miles would be affected, and the brilliance of the explosion could flashblind people 25 miles away. These bare facts cannot begin to describe what would be experienced by even those on the outer borders of the blast zone. The first visible effect would be a flash of light so bright that even the reflection would cause flashblindness, and severe second degree burns would occur on exposed flesh. Then a blast wave would follow which would destroy all before it, until with dissipated energy it would blow in windows 10 miles away, uproot trees, but leave some houses repairable in peacetime conditions. Then, depending on the height of the burst above the ground there could be a rainout of radioactive products. Major radioactivity would only be expected as a consequence of a ground burst, in which case a proportion of the blast would be absorbed by the earth, which would become contaminated with radioactivity and blasted into the atmosphere, leaving a large crater.

The consequences of a 1 megaton ground-burst explosion for any people caught in it range from a 98% death rate within 2 miles, 50% from 2 to 2.5 miles, to 5% at 6 miles. Even as far as 9 miles out a 25% injury rate could be expected (Office of Technology Assessment, 1980).

These figures are for the immediate consequences only, and are lower than the three month survival rates, which will include the deaths of the untreated wounded from injury, infection, malnutrition and exposure. These matters cannot be discussed here, but fuller accounts can be found elsewhere (*BMA Report*, 1983; IPPNW, 1982; AMBIO, 1983).

Nuclear weapon stockpiles

There is general agreement that the total number of nuclear bombs exceeds 50,000 (SIPRI, 1982). Eighteen and a half thousand of these are bombs capable of being delivered by planes and missiles to intercontinental targets (SIPRI, 1984). The rest have shorter ranges, though there is considerable flexibility in the use of many of these weapons. A fully loaded missile may have a short range, yet have a very much longer range if fitted with only one warhead. The classification of weapons into supposedly distinct categories is highly questionable, since in the heat of war many improvised methods could be utilized to deliver the bombs to their targets.

Likely targets in Britain

Every nuclear power makes plans as to where it will drop its bombs, and the general outlines of these are known. The priority targets are the nuclear weapons of potential enemies, followed by conventional military targets such as airfields, headquarters and communication centres. Then follow targets which make it difficult for a nation to sustain long-term warfare, such as ports, industrial centres connected with war industries, nuclear and conventional power stations. It is assumed that the deliberate destruction of civilian populations is not a priority.

On the basis of what is known about targeting policy it is possible to build up some possible scenarios of nuclear attack upon the United Kingdom. Openshaw, Steadman and Greene (1983) have carried out such a study. Their assessment will be used in this account, since it is the most detailed nationwide United Kingdom study of nuclear war effects. Assuming that a potential enemy follows the supposedly rational course of attempting to destroy military targets, then the likely casualties from the immediate effects of such an attack, amounting to about 215 megatons, will be roughly 35 million dead and about 5 million seriously injured. When the effects of smaller levels of attack are calculated, a linear increase in casualties is found, at a rough constant increase of about one casualty for every five tons of explosive equivalent. After about 215 megatons the casualty rate increases at a slower pace, since by then the attackers will literally be running out of people to kill. If on the other hand the potential attackers wished to maximize civilian casualties then 10 nuclear bombs on the most densely populated urban centres would kill and severely injure roughly 10 million people.

Immediate effects

The level of attack will have to be taken into consideration when estimating the likely psychological state of the survivors. The general expectation is that the greater the destruction, the harder it will be to apply the findings from current research into human disaster reactions to any nuclear survivors.

Examining the effects of varying weights of attack and calculating likely casualty figures depends on several important assumptions. The proportion of people assumed to be outdoors affects the numbers of burns cases, though this only appears to affect the total casualty rate once more than 30% of the population are assumed to be outdoors.

Wind direction is only important for low level attacks, since at higher levels the entire country is likely to be affected. The crucial assumption in the calculation of casualties is the amount of protection from radiation which buildings can be expected to afford their inhabitants. Optimistic assumptions can reduce the casualty rate by 5 millions in extreme cases, and official calculations seem to assume high levels of building protection. Most houses afford less protection than officially assumed, and will offer even less when damaged by blast. This factor is of greater significance than any assumptions about where, on the generally accepted range of 450 to 600 rads, the precise point of the lethal dose of radiation lies (Oppenshaw, Steadman and Greene, 1983).

Delayed effects

To every uncertainty about calculating the immediate casualties of nuclear attack must be added the greater uncertainties of determining the further deaths due to secondary consequences in the months to follow. In general, the prospects are not reassuring. An attack of over 200 megatons will totally destroy or severely damage 60% of the housing stock, and break every window in Britain. Oil tanker terminals are likely to be destroyed, which will severely restrict any surviving industry, assuming international trade still continues. The gas distribution systems would be non-functional and unsafe. Mine workings underground would be largely unaffected by the direct impact of the bombs, but would depend on intact power and electricity systems for ventilation and drainage, which would otherwise render pits unworkable. Electricity supplies would be disrupted by broken lines, by extensive damage to control systems brought about by electro-magnetic pulse, and by the destruction of generating stations. Deliberate targeting of nuclear power stations is highly likely, since these represent colossal material investments, and could potentially sustain power systems when conventional sources were cut off. Blast damage in the range 4 to 20 psi from a nearby bomb would be sufficient to damage air filters, auxiliary transformers and coolant pipes, which could in turn lead to a meltdown of the core with a release of its contents. A direct hit would distribute the radioactive material, containing isotopes such as Strontium 90 and Caesium 137 with extremely long half-lives, over a wide area. The effects of a bomb attack on unprotected nuclear waste tanks at Sellafield (Windscale) would lead to even longer term contamination.

Damage to industry would be severe, water supplies would be contaminated with fallout and sewage, total national uncontaminated food stocks would amount to less than a fortnight's supply, mechanized agriculture would be impossible without fuel, cattle and sheep would die at lower radiation dosage levels than humans, and trees would be blown down by blast (Oppenshaw, Steadman and Greene, 1983; AMBIO, 1983). The prospects for economic recovery without massive assistance from other undamaged industrialized nations would be very bleak.

Cultural damage, in the sense of the destruction of major libraries, universities and the architectural heritage of the nation, would further impoverish any surviving society, as well as denying it knowledge needed for recovery.

In addition, large scale nuclear war may reduce the quantity of ozone in the stratosphere (Petrov, 1983), and the effects of smoke from fires in the atmosphere could lead to marked reductions in sunlight for several weeks or longer, with marked reductions in temperature, and severe effects on climate and crops (Crutzen and Birks, 1983). Turco *et al.* (1983) have done detailed simulations of these effects under different assumptions about the extent of smoke and dust, and Alexandrov and Stenchikov (1983) describe a model which leads to similar conclusions. If these calculations are correct, then the long term global effects may be more damaging than the initial explosions themselves. As a matter of evidence, it is likely that considerable uncertainty will always remain in estimates of these global effects.

Conclusions

Attacks of the sort considered likely by military planners will create damage so extensive as to destroy a functioning civilization in the United Kingdom. This strains to the upper limit any calculations which can be made as to likely psychological reactions. Even a few nuclear bombs on urban centres would constitute the worst catastrophe the nation has experienced since the Black Death.

2

REACTIONS TO DISASTER

No disaster experienced in recorded history resembles the potential destruction of major nuclear war. Nonetheless, past disasters can give us pointers to the likely responses of those who survive the immediate effects, though it will always be necessary to interpret the findings carefully with due allowance for the differences which restrict the applicability of the comparison.

Localized disasters such as explosions and fires give a partial view of likely reactions, which in the case of nuclear war would be repeated across whole continents. Earthquakes and floods give a better understanding of large scale and generalized destruction, though it is correspondingly more difficult to comprehensively evaluate how everyone reacted. All these disasters differ from the nuclear case in that there is always an undamaged outside world able to offer some help and assistance. Further, the imponderable effects of radiation will impose a delay on rescue attempts, since most people will be unable to establish when it is safe to come out from what remains of their shelter. Electromagnetic pulse is likely to have severely damaged the communication networks on which all effective relief operations depend. Most of all, the likely extent of the physical destruction to civilization would be so extensive as to make unlikely any concerted rescue operation, even if it could be mounted. Most people would be concerned with their own survival and the 'illusion of centrality' which is held by disaster victims would for many be more of a reality than an illusion. Most people would feel that they were at the centre of the catastrophe, and would have some basis for that view, since most would have experienced damage and injury, though the extent of the damage would depend on the distance from the centre of the explosion.

Section 1. The analysis of human reactions to disasters

Although past disasters are imperfect guides to the future they must be studied if likely future reactions are to be understood. Lievesley (1979) in a study on disasters and welfare planning gives over 400 references, Kinston and Rosser (1974) give 117, and Churcher *et al.* (1981) have reviewed the literature with reference to nuclear war.

Kinston and Rosser (1974) reviewed the psychological effects of disasters, which they define as situations of massive collective stress, attempting to draw some conclusions from the extensive but unsystematized literature on human reactions to catastrophes. They note that there has often been a reluctance to investigate these reactions fully, as if researchers were averting their eyes from what they found. It was 17 years before any attempt was made to study the psychological consequences of the bombings of Hiroshima and Nagasaki. Even civil defence exercises set up to deal with simulated disasters fail to meet the pressing psychological needs of the supposed victims, and reveal an apparent unwillingness to confront the misery of personal tragedy. In the Hartford Disaster Exercise (Menczer, 1968) it was found that rescue personnel became confused and disturbed by the sight of massive injuries and this led to the 'victims' being placed in uncomfortable and dangerous positions. At no time did anyone stay with a specific victim to give comfort and reassurance, though these are desperately needed by the victims.

Even when prompt and effective treatment is available, as in the burns victims described by Cobb and Lindemann (1944), and despite excellent planning and precautions to minimize psychological stress, 43% of the survivors of the fire showed evidence of psychiatric illness. This indicates the pressing need to investigate as fully as possible how people react to disasters, and to be aware of the psychological impairment which usually results.

Despite a measure of reluctance to investigate the consequences of catastrophes, some features have been identified. Kinston and Rosser use a classification system based on the work of Tyhurst (1951) and Glass (1959), who categorize the phases of disaster as: threat, warning, impact, recoil and post-impact. Although these categories merely represent points along a dimension, and describe average reactions which may not occur in all people, they help us understand the course of events.

The sequence of events

(i) Threat

All life is subject to potential hazards, but some are more evident and dangerous than others. Earthquake belts, volcanic slopes, war zones and flood plains all carry particular risks. In terms of the risk of nuclear war, countries which themselves deploy nuclear weapons are especially at risk, and within those countries missile bases and possibly urban centres are likely targets. The evaluation of risk is a problematic subject, involving subjective estimates and attempts to calculate probabilities. Slovic and Fischoff (1980) have looked at public perceptions of a variety of hazards, and have shown that perceived risks are often at variance with actual risks. These differences may be partly accounted for by the prominence which the media give to dramatic events, thus increasing their salience over less newsworthy occurrences. Eiser and Van der Pligt (1979, 1983) have shown that the evaluation of the risks of nuclear power accidents is influenced by general positive or negative attitudes to nuclear power in terms of potential social benefits. Lee (1981) and Lee, Brown and Henderson (1984) have argued that such comparisons of public perceptions with mortality statistics give an unfair impression of irrationality. Indeed, Slovic, Fishchoff and Lichtenstein (1982) have shown that when both experts and members of the public are asked to rate hazards by other perceived characteristics such as the extent of catastrophic potential and whether the risk is voluntary, then much of the difference between the two groups disappears. Britten (1983) has conducted a major review on the risk of nuclear war, and shown it to be higher than is generally publicly admitted.

Threat is the condition under which we live at present. It is evident that a pressing danger exists, but the perceived salience of the threat will vary from person to person and time to time. Chivian (1983) has reviewed children's sense of nuclear threat, and argues that this is more widespread and substantial than generally realized. Escalona (1963, 1965, 1982) has extensively studied children's and adolescents' fears about nuclear war, fears which she feels threaten their belief in the future and the trustworthiness of their parents. Schwebel (1982) suggests that the nuclear threat is a contributing factor in anxiety and other disorders noted among teenagers. Beardslee and Mack (1982) conclude that children are deeply disturbed by the threat of nuclear war, and have doubts about their own survival. In the United Kingdom 52% of teenagers feel that nuclear war will occur in their lifetime, and 70% that it is inevitable one day (Business Decisions, 1983). Tizard (1984) reviewed the literature on children's fears about nuclear war. She found that many of the studies were unsystematic, but that methodologically sound studies, which had asked large representative samples of school leavers in the US neutral questions about the future, found increasing levels of alarm about the nuclear threat. Bachman (1984) in such a study found that the proportion of adolescents often worried about the nuclear threat rose from 7% in 1976 to 31% in 1982, and the feeling that nuclear or biological annihilation would occur in their lifetimes rose from 23% in 1976 to 35% in 1982.

Solantous *et al.* (1984) in a survey of 5000 Finnish 12 to 18-year-olds found that even in this non-nuclear neutral country 79% of the 12-year-olds and 48% of the 18-year-olds named a probable future war as their major fear. Adults share this concern, and show a general perception that they are at risk because of nuclear weapons, though this is rarely stated as the most pressing worry people face. In 1982 a Gallup poll found that 72% of an adult sample were worried about nuclear war and 38% thought that nuclear war would occur.

In general there is no consistent relationship between such anxieties and attitudes to nuclear weapons policies. Despite evidence of anxiety in many people, the most consistent reaction appears to be some form of denial, which Lifton (1967) describes as 'consistent human adaptation'. Some people avoid the subject totally. Other reactions are resignation, helplessness (Seligman, 1975), fatalism and unquestioning trust. The myth of personal invulnerability, that necessary fiction of everyday life, holds strong, and allows people to continue the necessary tasks of living. All authority tends to be displaced onto leaders and authorities, and people tend to feel helpless and unable to influence events through their actions.

(ii) Warning

Simply because a warning has been given it does not mean that it will be heeded. Denial can continue in some individuals up to the moment of impact itself. During the Hawaiian tidal wave of May 1960 evacuation was minimal (Lachman, Tatsuoka and Bank, 1961), and on the banks of the Rio Grande festive crowds watched and cheered the rising floodwaters (Wolfenstein, 1957). These active denials of danger have their place in everyday life, but when they are carried over in the face of a real threat they constitute a danger in themselves, since they obstruct preventive action. The myth of personal invulnerability still holds. A measure of this delusion may be gauged by the finding that the majority of people believe they are more likely than average to live past 80 years of age (Britten, 1983).

Once the danger has been admitted then, in those who are trusting, an over-reliance on official pronouncements may result, with susceptibility to rumour being the case for those who lack faith in parental establishment figures. Precautionary activity depends on the adequacy of information as to what needs to be done, and a group effect as people begin to take the warning seriously. Conflicting advice is usual (Churcher *et al.*, 1981), and many people may be unable to decide upon a consistent response.

(iii) Impact

When disasters are sudden and severe, most people feel that they are at the very centre of the catastrophe. This illusion of centrality, though understandable, may prevent optimum responses since most people will concern themselves with their own local problems. In a tornado people believe that only their house has been hit. The myth of personal invulnerability, which is so strong in the threat phase, is now called into question. Faced with the reality of death, usual assumptions disintegrate, and mood and beliefs oscillate wildly. As the full extent of the destruction becomes apparent, and help fails to materialize, there is the second shock effect of dismay at abandonment. Intense emotions are felt, and these fluctuate, making later recall of events problematical. Feelings fluctuate between terror and elation, invulnerability and helplessness, catastrophic abandonment and miraculous escape. All survivors must attempt to make sense of the fact that they could have died, and nearly died, but managed to come through alive. They show the exhilaration of massive anxiety relief, but also the vulnerability to disappointment which is the longer-term effect of the massive fear they have experienced. Joy at having survived may be mixed with colossal optimism that the worst is over. Life itself seems sufficient reward, and in particular joining up with loved ones, who were feared lost, brings intense happiness. The quite random fact of survival may be rationalized by a feeling of personal invulnerability and mission. Those who have had a brush with death are left in a heightened state of emotional turmoil.

This effect is short-lived, and soon gives way to the 'disaster syndrome'. Victims appear dazed, stunned and bewildered (Wallace, 1956). Contrary to popular belief, their reactions are not the ones associated with panic. Quarantelli (1954) describes panic as an acute fear reaction, developing as a result of a feeling of entrapment, powerlessness and isolation, leading to nonsensical and irrational flight behaviour. Such frenzied activity is only found when people are trapped, and when escape is thought possible only for a limited period of time. Then contagious panic can indeed occur, but it is not the norm in disasters.

After a disaster victims are apathetic, docile, indecisive, unemotional, and they behave mechanically. They are still in a state of high autonomic arousal, but appear to be paying for their period of terror by emotional and behavioural exhaustion. Various explanations have been put forward for this passive response. It may be a protective reaction, cutting people off from further stimuli which would only cause them anxiety and pain. In an account of the Tokyo earthquake of 1894 Balz noted that he observed the terrible event 'with the same cold attention with which one follows an absorbing physical experiment...all the higher affective life was extinguished' (cited in Anderson, 1942). Again, it could be a form of wishful fantasy – 'if I don't react then nothing has happened'. Or it could be that people feel helpless in the face of the massive damage and the impossibility of repairing their shattered world. Whatever the reason, the survivor is left in a diminished condition, and is highly vulnerable. Guilt feelings are common, since the catastrophe will have released unacceptable egotistical feelings, including excitement at the deaths of others. Fear will have prevented people from helping others, leaving survivors with only the fantasy of the heroism they would have liked to have shown in the emergency. Even within families, some will have put their own safety above those of other family members.

Popovic and Petrovic (1964) arrived on the scene of the Skopije earthquake 22 hours after the event, and in the following five days, together with a team of local psychiatrists, toured the evacuation camps. They found that much of the population was in a mild stupor, depressed, congregating in small unstable groups and prone to rumours of doom. Prompt outside help, responsible and informative reporting by the press, and the speedy evacuation of the more disturbed victims all contributed to an eventual return to apparent psychological normality. By way of comparison with nuclear war, it should be noted that only 1 in 200 of the people died, and 3 in 200 were injured, far less than would be expected in a nuclear explosion. In any disaster, according to Kinston and Rosser's (1974) estimates, although roughly three-quarters of the population are likely to show the disaster syndrome, anywhere from 12% to 25% will be tense and excited, but able to cope by concentrating on appropriate preparatory activities. They will be capable of making themselves too busy to worry, though their activities may often be of only marginal relevance to the threat they face. At times of stress overlearned familiar routines can serve as a solace. Equally, 12% to 25% will fare far worse, and will show grossly inappropriate behaviour, with anxiety symptoms predominating. There will be an immediate increase in psychological distress, as those already vulnerable are triggered into breakdown. Such effects are more likely for reactive disorders than those which are psychotic in origin. Those whose behaviour is contained only by social pressure are likely to behave in psychopathic ways. The crisis will provide an opportunity which some will be willing to exploit.

(iv) Recoil

If the cause of the disaster is seen to pass, and some sort of 'all clear' can be announced, then there will be an opportunity for a return to something approximating a normal psychological state. About 90% of subjects show a return of awareness and recall. They are highly dependent, talkative, childlike, seeking safety and forming unstable social groups. In this state they remain highly vulnerable and emotionally labile. Some respond with totally psychopathic behaviour, and looting, rape, and heavy drinking may occur. People show a return of energy with a commensurate return of reason. They behave hyperactively and often irrationally. They become obsessed with communicating their experiences to others and need to work through the events in order to give them some meaning. The need for explanation is part of dependency, and leads to rumour and absurd gullibility. People will be anxious to obtain reliable news, and will expect their own experiences to be news. Monitoring the news serves as an attempt to reconstruct a comprehensible set of explanations, and to reduce the uncertainty brought about by uncontrollability. For example, following the murder of President Kennedy the average US adult spent eight hours per day for the next four days listening to the radio or watching television, behaviour which Janis (1971) interpreted as an attempt to work through the cultural damage.

In this dependent and vulnerable state, chance factors can have a disproportionate effect on the interpretation of the event and the view as to what has to be done in the future. Scapegoats may need to be found, and chance may provide them. Scientists, militarists and politicians may escape initial attention while those involved in bringing relief may be the target of frustration and feelings of betrayal (Lacey, 1972).

Once the immediate danger is past, some survivors will begin to take steps to cope with the consequences. Even as the warning of danger is announced people will find themselves in a conflict of roles. They will have to decide whether they should continue with their jobs, take up civic and emergency duties or return to look after their families. Killian (1952) found that conflicting group loyalties and contradictory roles were significant factors affecting individual behaviour in critical situations. Typically, it is the person without family ties who leads rescue work, while the others generally run to their homes to discover if their families are in danger. Even so, Killian reported that some who were searching for their families, after a tornado had struck, were capable of helping others they found on the way. Those whose occupational roles bore little relationship to the needs created by the disaster, such as shopkeepers, disregarded their jobs more easily and came to the assistance of the community.

Faced with an overwhelming catastrophe family bonds are likely to predominate over civic duties, because everyday tasks and responsibilities will be seen as irrelevant and futile by most people. It should be noted that natural disasters generally come without warning, and rarely require emergency workers to leave their families unprotected while moving themselves to places of relative safety, as would apparently be required of them in the event of nuclear war. Such a dilemma would impose a severe additional stress upon the people concerned.

(v) Post-impact

Gradually, individual reactions become coordinated into an organized social response. The form this will take depends very much on cultural norms. Many of the victims will be coping with the consequences of loss and bereavement. This will diminish their capacity to interact socially in a productive manner. Victims need some form of acknowledgement of their suffering, but social norms may deny them the right to express their grief and hopelessness. Fear and apprehension persist, and many may feel that the catastrophe will recur. Aftershocks of an earthquake commonly cause more fear than the initial shock itself. People develop a conditioned fear response, and their capacity to maintain control of their emotions is diminished. Disaster persists as a tormenting memory, and is relived again and again.

Section 2. Reactions of special groups

Children

Studies of the effects on children of bombardment during World War II indicate that children show acute disturbance, which is worst in the 8 to 12-year age range, and worst in those with previous disorder and those from unstable homes. Anxiety and fear, predominantly of being separated from parents; restlessness, irritability, dependent and demanding behaviour, disturbance of bodily functions and difficulty in concentration are the major effects (Edwards, 1976). In the early aftermath of the disaster, children show compulsive patterns of behaviour. Popovic and Petrovic (1964) found that after the Skopije earthquake, the favourite play of children was based on the earthquake itself and the burial of bodies.

If parents have been able to cope during the crisis, and can create an accepting atmosphere in which fears can be expressed, then children appear to be psychologically fairly resilient. If parents are unable to cope, then children will mirror parental distress, and their recovery is likely to be slow.

In a major review of stress, coping and development, Rutter (1981) notes that one of the major determinants of a child's reaction to hospitalization is the parents' level of anxiety. A calm and coping parent can help a child deal with the anxieties which are intrinsic to hospital procedures. Rutter also notes that frightening events *per se*, without personal connotations of loss, are less likely to provoke psychiatric disorder that those with persisting consequences in terms of altered personal relationships or negative self-appraisal.

The elderly

The elderly tend to receive warnings later than other people, are less willing to leave their homes, tend to restrict their attention to their immediate family, are vulnerable to physical injury, but are resigned and show brief episodes of agitated depression and confusion (Kinston and Rosser, 1974). The elderly experience a much deeper sense of deprivation and loss than the rest of the community (Friedsam, 1961). They feel the loss of material possessions, particularly their homes, keenly, since these are familiar supports in their lives which cannot be replaced. In a sense, they feel that time has been destroyed, their remaining days despoiled, and they are left with a permanent sense of loss (Edwards, 1976).

The mentally ill

Some mentally ill patients may show dramatic improvements in coping ability and behaviour, but these are transient, and disappear as the emergency response fades. Neurotic hospitalized patients generally behave rationally, severely agitated patients become more excited, and those being treated for drug dependence steal drugs or abscond (Koegler and Hicks, 1972). Depending on the extent of the disaster the standard of care may be lowered, with a consequent deterioration in the condition of inpatients, and reduced services for the new casualties of the disaster.

Relief workers and hospital staff

Nurses are placed under stress by worry about the safety of their own families, and particularly when many children are injured, the emotional demands are extremely high. Nurses expect to work to a high standard, and the pressure of many injured patients to be cared for, lack of supplies, disorganization, increased responsibility and excessive demands make this difficult. In general, nursing staff can cope in the short term if the rest of the health system continues to function. Surgeons and physicians are not immune from emotional reactions to disaster victims, but may sometimes downplay the emotional needs of their patients (Edwards, 1976).

In general, relief workers find that any way of translating their sense of urgency into action reduces their own anxiety, though these actions may not always be entirely effective.

Section 3. **Long-term effects**

(i) Bereavement

Since bereavement is a common consequence of disasters, it is helpful to understand some of the features of grief in normal circumstances, uncomplicated by the further disruption of the disaster itself. Although these reactions vary from person to person, they present an additional burden to the survivor, though the normal pattern of grieving may be distorted by the effects of the catastrophe on the individual.

Marris (1974) notes that although human beings are extremely adaptable, they tend to resist change, and to be disorientated by it when it occurs. Every person has an investment in maintaining a predictable environment, and most changes cause anxiety because they threaten loss of control. In his study of bereaved widows he lists the features of severe, normal grief as restlessness, inability to sleep, exhaustion, loss of appetite and a variety of somatic complaints. These widows found themselves acting as if their husbands were still alive, preparing meals, waiting for him to come back from work, thinking of news to tell him. The prevalent mood is apathy, sometimes leading to thoughts of suicide. The bereaved tend to withdraw from relationships, and often feel considerable guilt over remembered neglect or unkindness, or feel hostility against unhelpful doctors and an unfeeling world.

Murray Parkes (1965) and Gorer (1965) found closely similar

patterns of grief in their studies. The bereaved suffer physical distress and worse health, they cannot surrender the past, feel unable to comprehend their loss, and when the deaths they are grieving over are premature, are particularly prone to hostility and guilt. The time course of grief is typically about two years. After the numbness of the first shock has worn off, the pain and distress become more severe and persist at this level for several weeks, gradually diminishing in intensity and severity over a year, with another year to run, on average, before reintegration with the community can occur. Although some recover sooner, many feel that the experience has permanently changed them and diminished their capacity to live fully. The bereaved lose not only their loved one but the meaning of their lives and any continuing sense of purpose.

After a major nuclear war even physically unharmed survivors would be likely to have lost close friends and relations, while those in the blast zone who survived injury are almost certain to have lost a loved one. The normal recovery from the acute phase of grief requires input and support from others. In the aftermath of a nuclear war such assistance is unlikely, since most of the survivors would be demanding support, rather than offering it. Grief reactions are likely to be more prolonged, and the level of impairment, usual in the bereaved under normal circumstances, considerably raised through a lack of social comfort and succour.

(ii) Long-term severe stresses

Although long-term stresses such as imprisonment in concentration camps and combat in war zones are particular man-made traumas, not natural disasters, they impose massive threat on their victims, and it is necessary to understand the psychological consequences of such events.

Studies of combat troops show that both acute and chronic reactions are the norm. Brill and Beebe (1955) in a study of 1000 cases of acute traumatic neurosis found that only the stress of combat and low educational attainment predicted the likelihood that troops showed 'battle fatigue'. Even willing, stable soldiers in units of high morale universally broke down if defeated or cut off. Kentsmith (1980) confirms that duration of stress is the most critical factor, and Swank (1949), studying 4000 survivors of the Normandy campaign, found that all soldiers became incapacitated once roughly three-quarters of their companions had been killed. These findings in highly trained young men show that faced with massive casualties and lack of support, effective behaviour is rarely possible.

The long-term consequences are not reassuring. Lidz (cited in Hocking, 1965) found that all survivors of the Guadalcanal evacuation developed neurotic symptoms in civilian life. Archibald *et al.* (1963) found that 15 years after the event 70% of the survivors suffered from chronic traumatic neurosis, one third were unemployed and another third only in unstable employment. Veterans are also more likely to show organic illness and higher death rates.

Kinston and Rosser (1974) review accounts of Nazi concentration camp survivors, since this gives another insight into the psychological effects of massive sustained stress and the everyday threat of death. The camps subjected the inmates to threatened and actual torture and death. Extreme cruelty had to be witnessed and endured without protest or sign of emotion. Violence was applied erratically, and no amount of good behaviour could save anyone from a capricious tormentor. In such impossible conditions of humiliation, threat and betrayal the main response was either apathy leading to eventual death or a degraded coping response, 'camp mentality', characterized by a selfish, compassionless, egotistical behaviour, centred on personal survival in the form of an absorption with food. After one detailed study of these concentration camps there was little published work on the survivors for about 15 years, and then studies began, eventually leading to an extensive literature. The survivor syndrome described is similar to post-traumatic neurosis, characterized by emotional tension, psychosomatic complaints, cognitive impairment, heightened vulnerability to stress, chronic depression with guilt and isolation. The condition is chronic, severe, and resistent to treatment, though only about 1% accept treatment at all. The failure of post-release Utopian dreams led either to helplessness or suspicion and mistrust. In terms later used by Seligman (1975), they had found that their behaviour did not affect outcomes, and reacted with learned helplessness and fatalism. Paradoxically, many made a good socio-economic recovery, as if some aspects of emotionless personal survival skills had been strengthened.

Section 4. **Case examples of disasters**

In order to estimate the probable psychological effects of nuclear war on the immediate physical survivors, studies of other catastrophes are helpful, but at the same time it must be understood how each differs from the effects of nuclear war. A few recent disasters will be described to illustrate features of reactions to disaster, and to serve as comparisons with the likely consequences of nuclear war.

(i) Buffalo Creek

On February 26th 1972 an enormous slag dam gave way and unleashed thousands of tons of water and black mud on the Buffalo Creek valley in southern West Virginia: 125 people died and 4000 were left homeless. Tichener and Kapp (1976) used observations of family interaction and psychoanalytically orientated individual interviews with survivors two years after the flood, and reported traumatic neurotic reactions in 80% of them. The underlying clinical picture was of unresolved grief, survivor shame and feelings of impotent rage and hopelessness. Erikson (1976) found that with the destruction of the community and the traditional supports of kinship and neighbourliness, survivors experienced demoralization, disorientation and loss of connection. They became apathetic and seemed to have forgotten how to care for one another. Erikson distinguished between individual trauma and social trauma. A road traffic victim who is looked after by the community suffers individual trauma, but in a large scale disaster all the victims suffer both. The close-knit mining community was destroyed, and people withdrew into themselves. A survivor reported:

> Each person in the family is a loner now, a person alone. Each of us
> is fighting his own battles. We just don't seem to care for each other
> anymore.

Erikson concluded that from the sociological point of view the people of Buffalo Creek were accustomed to placing their individual energies and resources at the disposal of the community, and then drawing from this communal store in times of need. When that store was destroyed they found that they could neither draw from nor invest in that social resource. They lacked all confidence and assurance, and found themselves almost empty of feeling and devoid of affection. In Erikson's metaphor of the social organism:

> It is as if the cells had supplied raw energy to the whole body but did
> not have the means to convert that energy into usable personal
> resources once the body was no longer there to process it.

This observation has important implications for the case of nuclear war, since social disruption is likely to be considerable among the survivors, and will severely restrict their capacity to rebuild a functioning society.

Rangell (1976) reported that the disaster was not unforeseen, but that people had attempted to put it out of their minds, and when the event occurred all their repressed fears immediately surfaced. The fact that they had been aware of the danger, could see the dam every day on the skyline, but had done nothing about it, contributed to their massive desolation when the feared event finally took place. Lifton and Olsen (1976) found that the complete destruction of the social community led to psychological impairment in all survivors studied two years after the flood. Despair, apathy and depression were common. Survivors had frequent memory lapses and confusion about events since the disaster, and many remained suspicious of offers of help. Some projected their anger onto the mining company, and all seemed to be trying to come to terms with the apparent lack of meaning of a disaster which had seemed to be preventable. In summary, the studies of the Buffalo Creek disaster reveal that substantial psychological impairment was inflicted on the survivors by the trauma of the event itself, and the accumulated effects of the loss of their supportive community.

(ii) Cyclone Tracy

On Christmas Eve 1974 Cyclone Tracy hit the town of Darwin in Northern Australia. By Christmas morning 50 people were dead and 90% of the housing had been destroyed. The population numbered 45,000, with a larger component of transient residents than other Australian cities, about 80% having been resident for less than a year; 28,000 were evacuated over the next few days, 20,000 of them by air. Parker (1977) administered the General Health Questionnaire, which lists a variety of physical and psychological complaints, to 67 evacuees who passed through a centre in Sydney five to eight days later. Background data collected on these respondents showed that before the cyclone only 15% reported poor physical health, poor nerves and unsatisfactory work . The reported concerns of the evacuees during the cyclone were the safety of other family members in 47% of cases, their own death in 30% and how best to protect themselves in 23%. Three subjects reported the death of a friend. Perhaps not suprisingly in this sample of evacuees, the most common preoccupation was a wish to get away from Darwin.

In terms of their responses to the questionnaire, 58% could be termed 'probable psychiatric cases', with most psychological disturbance being symptoms of anxiety or high arousal, loss of autonomy and mastery. Deep depression was rarely manifest. Six of the evacuees (9% of the sample) showed clear evidence of the 'disaster syndrome' characterized by dazed apathy, underactivity or aimless wandering, and their questionnaire scores reflected this, being two and a half times higher than the rest of the group.

A follow-up of these evacuees proved difficult, because they had by then dispersed over Australia. Only 48% returned questionnaires at 10 week follow-up, and only 27% at 14 month follow-up. Parker looked back at the original demographic data and found a decreasing sex ratio, but felt they were otherwise representative of the initial cohort in terms of age and initial psychological morbidity. However, extreme caution must be exercised when interpreting the follow-up results, since selective exclusion is likely on the part of these victims, and no interview or observation of their behaviour was carried out. At 10 weeks 41% of respondents showed scores high enough to classify them as 'probable psychiatric cases'. Among these 13 individuals were 4 whose initial scores had been normal. This suggests that many reactions develop over time, and that anxieties can 'incubate' in some individuals, appearing after the initial shock is over. At 14 months 22% showed scores above the cutoff point, which is at the population norm; 22% were still unemployed, which was far higher than the population norm, and doubted that things would ever be as good as they had been before the cyclone; 28% considered their nerves to be worse than before the cyclone, with 22% reporting an increase in anxiety symptoms and 11% depressive symptoms.

In summary, this study is a vivid example of the massive rescue response which is possible when undamaged areas vastly predominate over a localized disaster zone. More widespread damage throughout Australia would have diminished the capacity and even the willingness of other citizens to be helpful. There were no problems of contagion of disease, and no competition over food and resources to diminish altruistic responses. Sadly, no detailed interviewing or follow-up was achieved, but the initial findings confirm that there was a widespread and elevated anxiety response, and the suggestion is that this returned to quasi-normal levels after 14 months.

(iii) Three Mile Island

The accident at Three Mile Island is of particular interest because no deaths were caused nor was there any physical damage to personal property, but there was the threat of explosion and radioactive contamination (Kemeny, 1979; Perrow, 1984). Although the water pumps which failed at Three Mile Island Unit 2 at 4 am on 28th March 1979 initiated the accident, the emergency developed over the next few days, during which there were conflicting reports about the plant's safety. For the people in surrounding communities the emergency brought rumours, conflicting official statements, a lack of knowledge about radiation releases, the fear that a hydrogen bubble trapped inside the reactor might explode and the threat of mass evacuation. About 40%

of the population within 15 miles of the reactor were evacuated for five days on average. The main reasons for leaving were: the danger signalled by the appearance of the hydrogen bubble (30%), confusing information (19%) and the desire to avoid forced evacuation (14%) (Flynn and Chalmers, 1980). There was considerable distrust of the government's ability to provide satisfactory evacuation arrangements. Of those who stayed, one third gave fear of looting as a reason, possibly because looting had occurred in the district after a hurricane in 1972. None occurred during this emergency. Older people also stayed, and had a fatalistic attitude.

People distrusted the plant officials and federal authorities, and even pro-nuclear respondents felt that they were never truly made aware of the dangers of a nuclear power plant. The evacuation of schoolchildren was haphazard, and caused much distress to parents and children who had been separated. Evacuation of hospitals, psychiatric wards and prisons could not be carried out, and many workers such as ambulance drivers were placed in role conflict.

The psychological effects were felt most keenly by those within five miles of the reactor or with children near the reactor, and the strongest effect was demoralization, helplessness and depression. Survey data revealed that 25% of the population were showing such responses, where 15% was the population norm before the accident. Loss of appetite, difficulty in sleeping and irritability eventually passed, but a small percentage continued with somatic sypmtoms when contacted four months later.

A quarter of respondents still felt seriously threatened by the reactor four months later, and nine months later this was felt by between 10 to 20% of those within 15 miles of the reactor. Bromet (1980) found that mothers experienced an excess of clinical episodes of anxiety and depression during the year after the accident compared with control mothers outside the area.

Katz (1982) reports that all researchers were struck by a continually repeated fear expressed by people in the community – that they were being asked to deal with a danger they could not see, hear or feel. The event was beyond their experience, and no-one was seen as being sure how serious the accident was. Some of the researchers felt that since radiation hazard was invisible and outside ordinary experience, many citizens would be reluctant to rely on official pronouncements and would ignore advice in any potential nuclear emergency. Role conflicts were evident even for the well informed. In one hospital half of the nuclear medicine radiological staff evacuated themselves.

Hazards which are totally outside ordinary experience carry an additional burden of uncertainty and ambiguity. Radiation is not only invisible, but unstoppable in its consequences. In psychological terms, no safety signal is possible, since there is no way of knowing what injury has been sustained, and it may be many years before the full effects are felt.

Section 5. **The Black Death 1348-50**

No account of human reactions to disaster could be complete without a consideration of the effects on society of the most lethal disaster of recorded history, which killed an estimated one third of the population between India and Iceland. Tuchman (1978) has recounted the effects of the Black Death on Europeans of the fourteenth century, fully aware that people then lived under such different conditions and assumptions that no strict comparison with our age is possible. Yet despite the 600 year gap it remains the closest parallel to the disaster that could befall our own age, and if anything in that century seems familiar to us now, then it is likely to be those communalities of the human spirit which supersede cultural and material differences. Tuchman quotes an historian who compared the aftermaths of the Black Death with the First World War and found all the same complaints:

> economic chaos, social unrest, high prices, profiteering, depraved
> morals, lack of production, industrial indolence, frenetic gaiety,
> wild expenditure, luxury, debauchery, social and religious hysteria,
> greed, avarice, maladministration, decay of manners (op. cit.).

History never repeats itself, but man always does, Voltaire asserted. Despite the difficulties inherent in drawing firm conclusions from a disaster in a different age, we cannot afford to ignore what evidence we have about this event.

   Tuchman based her account on the considerable records of the time on births, deaths, taxes, wages, agricultural production and laws and regulations, rather than simply literary accounts. Bubonic plague made its first appearance in Europe in October 1347. It was present in two forms: one carried in the bloodstream, causing internal bleeding and swellings in the armpits and the groin, which was spread by contact and killed within five days; and a more virulent pneumonic type, which infected the lungs and was spread by respiratory infection and killed within one to three days. The disease was so lethal that there were known cases of people who went to sleep apparently well, and died before they woke. Rumours of a plague from the East which had depopulated India had arrived in 1346. By January 1348 it had reached

Marseille and then, spread by boats along coasts and navigable rivers, reached Avignon in March, Paris by June and southern England by August. The plague killed over a four-month period before moving on, except in large cities where it abated over winter and then reappeared in spring for a further six months. It travelled as far north as Iceland and Greenland and eventually abated in Europe by mid-1350. As far as can be judged from all the available data 'a third of the world died'. People said and believed that this was the end of the world.

In contrast to the effects of nuclear war, the physical structure of civilization was left intact, though with a diminished population agricultural production fell, thus leading to a further fall in population as successive waves of plague savaged an enfeebled, malnourished population.

The main psychological effects, as deduced from contemporary accounts and art, were a massive pessimism, a lack of confidence and a profound sense of the misery of life. Fields were left untilled, ripe wheat was left uncut, cattle were allowed to stray, and enterprise and innovation seemed worthless. With so few hands remaining to restore the work of centuries people felt the world would never regain its former prosperity. The cathedral at Siena, planned to be the largest in the world, was abandoned, and work never resumed, leaving the truncated transept where it still stands 'in permanent witness to the sweep of death's scythe' (Tuchman, p. 96).

The official investigation into the causes of the plague drew on the astrological theories of the day, and concluded that an unfavourable conjunction of planets had been responsible. This explanation seemed as far-fetched to the population then as it must seem to us today. The people drew on their own system of beliefs, and concluded that they had been punished for having sinned. To Piers Plowman 'these pestilences were for pure sin'. (This same response was observed in the victims of a volcanic eruption in contemporary Mexico, where the villagers used precisely the same notion of punishment and sin.)

The post-plague medieval world responded in ways which would now be characterized as profoundly disturbed. Flagellants and cultists achieved new status and increased followings. Scapegoats were searched for and found in the Jewish community, who were the victims of pogroms. Rumours of all sorts circulated through the disturbed and anxious community.

Emotional response, dulled by the horrors which had been experienced, underwent a kind of atrophy, and it was chronicled that there 'was burying without sorrow and wedding without friendschippe' (Tuchman, 1978, p.96).

Yet, despite the catastrophe, much of life continued. Dying of plague, tenants continued to pay their dues. The marriage rate rose, but mostly for financial advantage now that there were so many orphans who had inherited property. There was a great moving around, as peasants moved into empty rich houses, and ate off silver plate. Prices fell, and people spent while they could. Behaviour grew more reckless and callous, and there was much litigation over property rights.

The population level fell further over the rest of the century with successive waves of plague. Whole villages disappeared and cleared land was reclaimed by the wilderness. The archives of the Abbey of Ramsay show that 30 years after the plague the acreage of grain was less than half what it had been before. As death slowed production, manufactured goods became scarce and prices soared. Workers agitated for higher wages and met with official repression. The usual roles and certainties of the medieval world were shaken, and people were left in apprehension, tension and gloom.

Looked at from the perspective of our present age, the explanatory systems used in the medieval world appear strange, but the behaviour described is uncomfortably familiar. Contagion does not make for altruism, nor can one expect charitable behaviour from those who have survived so terrible an experience. The Black Death differed from the nuclear threat we face in this century in that the physical world was left intact, and the onset of the catastrophe was somewhat slower. However, the punishing long-term effect on the mood of the survivors is clear even across the gap of six centuries, providing a distant mirror for our own time.

Brother John Clyn kept a record of all that happened to him and his fellow friars lest 'things which should be remembered perish with time and vanish from the memory of those who come after us'. Waiting for death, he wrote 'I leave parchment to continue this work, if perchance any man survive and any of the race of Adam escape this pestilence and carry on the work which I have begun.' The record was completed in another hand.

Section 6. **Nuclear disasters: Hiroshima and Nagasaki**

The bombings of Hiroshima and Nagasaki offer a partial view of the effects of a potential future nuclear war. The weapons were very small by present day standards, the culture and the age were different, and there was neither warning nor any knowledge of radiation. The Hiroshima bomb, at about the equivalent of 12,500 tons of TNT, would now be regarded as a small battlefield weapon or merely as the detonator of a one megaton strategic bomb. However, these bombings are still the closest examples of what would occur in a contemporary nuclear war, with larger explosions on a potential 18,500 strategic targets (SIPRI, 1984).

Considering the importance for our age of these events, the bombings of Hiroshima and Nagasaki have been underreported. Some accounts have been often repeated, but much of the film material collected at the time has only recently been released, and the work done with the survivors was incomplete and often exaggeratedly technical, avoiding personal accounts and bypassing a mass readership.

Lifton (1967) picked 33 survivors at random from lists kept by local Hiroshima research institutes, plus 42 who were particularly articulate or prominent in the A-bomb problem. A structured interview explored the individual's recollection of the original experience and its meaning in the present as well as residual concerns and fears, and the meaning of his or her identity as a survivor.

The survivors were submitted without warning to an explosion so vast that it seemed that the world itself was coming to an end. At 8.15 am on 6 August 1945 most people in Hiroshima were in a relaxed state, since the all-clear had just sounded. Few people could recall their initial perceptions, some seeing the 'pika', a flash of light, or feeling a wave of heat, and some hearing the 'don', the thunder of the explosion, depending on where they were at the moment of impact. Everyone assumed that a bomb had fallen out of a clear sky directly on them, and they were suddenly and absolutely shifted from normal existence to an overwhelming encounter with death, a theme which stayed with each survivor indefinitely (Lifton, 1963). Those far from the city were shocked to see that Hiroshima had ceased to exist. A young university professor, 2500 metres from the hypocentre at the time summed up those feelings of weird, awesome unreality in a frequently expressed image of hell:

> Everything I saw made a deep impression – a park nearby covered with dead bodies waiting to be cremated...very badly injured people evacuated in my direction...Perhaps the most impressive thing I saw were girls, very young girls, not only with their clothes torn off but their skin peeled off as well...My immediate thought was that this was like the hell I had always read about...I had never seen anything which resembled it before, but I thought that should there be a hell, this was it.

In Nagasaki a young doctor Akizuki (1981) was preparing to treat a patient when the atom bomb exploded. After pulling himself from the debris of his Urakami hospital consulting room, he was eventually able to look out of where the window had been to the world outside.

> The sky was dark as pitch, covered with dense clouds of smoke; under that blackness, over the earth, hung a yellow-brown fog. Gradually the veiled ground became visible, and the view beyond rooted me to the spot with horror. All the buildings I could see were on fire...Electricity poles were wrapped in flame like so many pieces of kindling. Trees on the near-by hills were smoking, as were the leaves of sweet potatoes in the fields. To say that everything burned is not enough. The sky was dark, the ground was scarlet, and in between hung clouds of yellowish smoke. Three kinds of colour – black, yellow and scarlet – loomed ominously over the people, who ran about like so many ants seeking to escape. What had happened? Urakami hospital had not been bombed – I understood that much. But that ocean of fire, that sky of smoke! It seemed like the end of the world. (Akizuki, 1981)

After encountering so much horror, survivors found that they were incapable of emotion. They behaved mechanically, felt emotionally numb, and at the same time knew they were partly trying to pretend to be unaffected in a vain attempt to protect themselves from the trauma of what they were witnessing.

> I went to look for my family. Somehow I became a pitiless person, because if I had pity I would not have been able to walk through the city, to walk over those dead bodies. The most impressive thing was the expression in people's eyes – bodies badly injured which had turned black – their eyes looking for someone to come and help them. They looked at me and knew I was stronger than they...I was looking for my family and looking carefully at everyone I met to see if he or she was a family member – but the eyes – the emptiness – the helpless expression – were something I will never forget. (Lifton, 1963)

A businessman who had hastily semi-repaired his son's shoe before he went to work in the city centre was overcome with guilt that this same shoe had prevented his child from fleeing the fire. The man fruitlessly searched for his child's body, and was left in a state of perpetual self-accusation.

Most survivors focused on one ultimate horror which had left them with a profound sense of pity, guilt or shame. A baby still half-alive on his dead mother's breast, loved ones abandoned in the fire, pathetic requests for help which had to be ignored - each survivor carried a burning memory.

In Nagasaki Akizuki was swamped by burnt survivors clamouring for water and medical attention.

> Half naked or stark naked, they walked with strange, slow steps, groaning from deep inside themselves as if they had travelled from the depths of hell. They looked whitish; their faces were like masks. I felt as if I were dreaming, watching pallid ghosts processing slowly in one direction – as in a dream I had once dreamt in my childhood.

Severely injured people cried out for help. Parents refused to leave dead children, still requesting that they be attended by the doctor. Passing planes caused panic, and victims tried to hide till they passed. Most survivors had witnessed terrible scenes, piles of dead bodies heaped up in streams, mothers and children locked in each other's arms, a mother and her foetus still connected by its umbilical cord, all dead (Akizuki, 1981).

The recreation of the bombings, even 17 years later, caused the interviewees intense emotion, bringing back to them:

> an indelible imprint of death immersion which has formed the basis of a permanent encounter with death, a fear of annihilation of self and individual identity along with the sense of having virtually experienced the annihilation, the destruction of the non-human environment, of the field or context of one's existence and so of one's being-in-the-world, and replacement of the natural order of living and dying with an unnatural order of death-dominated life.
> (Lifton, 1963)

These survivors were so profoundly affected by what they had experienced that all aspects of their subsequent lives were marked by it, and they felt that they had come into contact with death but remained alive. Survivors attempt to make sense of the fact that they have survived whilst others have perished. Unable to accept that this was a chance occurrence survivors are convinced that their survival was made possible by the deaths of others, and this conviction causes them terrible guilt. Guilt and shame developed very quickly in Hiroshima survivors, as it did in those who escaped concentration camps, and in both cases it has been intense and persistent. Lifton set out the train of thought of Hiroshima survivors thus:

> I was almost dead...I should have died...I did die or at least am not alive...or if I am alive it is impure of me to be so...anything which I do which affirms life is also impure and an insult to the dead who alone are pure...and by living as if dead, I take the place of the dead and give them life.

This is the painful accommodation which the holocaust survivor makes to the joyless fact of having survived. It is grief made the more keen by there being no bodies to be buried and mourned, nor any familiar landmarks to show that life continues, and thus aid adjustment to loss. Person, body, house, street, city and even nature itself have been consumed.

Three persistent rumours circulated in Hiroshima just after the bomb. The first was that for 75 years the area would be uninhabitable, the second that trees and grass would never grow there again, and the third that all those who had been exposed to the bomb would be dead within three years. All these rumours contain understandable fears about contamination and the lingering effects of radiation. The fear remained with many victims permanently, being boosted by the outbreaks of radiation-induced leukaemia five years later. Every minor ailment is perceived as a potential indicator of personal doom.

Survivors felt that they were forced into a special category, the 'hibakusha', a stigmatized and forsaken group. The taint of death they carry makes others turn away, and forces the survivors to identify with the dead. They feel they are guinea pigs, victims of an experiment on which data are still being collected. When new life returns from the outside it is alien, uncomfortable and only serves to highlight how things have changed and how much has been lost.

To the newcomers the survivors are an embarassment, who make them feel guilty of usurpation, and to whom they respond with ostracism and resentment. The survivors themselves resent charitable attention, but also crave it. They are discriminated against socially and in business because of fears of contamination and delayed illness. Once the post-disaster Utopia collapses all these conflicts come to the fore, and they leave the survivors locked in a spiral of grief and resentment, which for many becomes a paranoid response. This attitude further inhibits their integration into the new community, who prefer to honour the dead than deal with the living. This leads to such sad events as survivors with skin burns being asked not to use public swimming pools (Lifton, 1967).

Although proper follow up studies of psychological effects do not appear to have been done, psychotic disorder is uncommon, but depression and anxiety about cancer, fears of death and dying, and generalized complaints of fatigue, dizziness, irritability and difficulty in coping are usual. This pattern is similar to that found after major civil disturbances, and could be conceptualized as an understandable concentration of the attention on possible danger signals to the exclusion of long-term plans. The absence of proper follow-up studies is itself a psychological phenomenon worthy of note, since it suggests that the scientific community itself averted its eyes from the long-term consequences of the disaster.

In Lifton's view the experience of the atomic bombings differed from other disasters in that it plunged the survivors into an interminable and unresolvable encounter with death. The immediate horrifying carnage was followed by long-term delayed effects, thus breaking the myth of personal invulnerability in a permanent way. In experiential terms, every victim saw their secure sunlit world destroyed in an instant. It felt like the end of the world, not just the end of one city. It is not hard to understand why they should distrust the apparent 'all-clear'.

Summary and conclusions

Understanding the effects of a possible nuclear war depends upon judging which of our past disasters offers the best mirror to the future. A sudden catastrophic destruction is likely to reduce the future functioning of the survivors more than gradual and sustained stress, since those who get through that will still have some survival skills left. It is evident that the common feature in both the A-bomb survivors and the concentration camp inmates was the existence of an outside world of helpers with resources and some wish to assist their recovery. Neither of these could be guaranteed after a major nuclear war.

Catastrophes subject those who survive them to severe psychological stress, and the magnitude of this effect has been calculated by Kinston and Rosser (1974), using data derived from the work of Brown *et al.* (1973) on the relationship between life events and subsequent mental illness. They calculate that the incidence of depressive illness could increase threefold and neurotic illness tenfold. These estimates assume that there is a functioning society to which the victims can return for support and assistance.

Chazov and Vartanian (1983) have attempted to calculate the effects on human behaviour of nuclear war, and are convinced that need for care would outstrip the psychiatric facilities in the Soviet Union 50 times over. Anxiety, fear, irritability and confusion are the expected immediate reactions. Assuming that about 20 to 25% of the European urban population survive the immediate effects of bombing, then Chazov and Vartanian expect that at least one third of the survivors will suffer from severe mental and behavioural disturbance, mostly acute anxiety, and that 20% of the survivors will be so incapacitated as to be unable to care for themselves or others.

None of the catastrophes so far experienced can match the conditions which are likely to be created by a major nuclear war. As previously noted, the large scale and general destruction will make rescue operations highly unlikely, and the effects of radiation will further impair people's willingness to come out to assist fellow victims. The economic, social and possibly climatic disruption will severely reduce people's capacity for recovery. The calculations above, and the findings on recovery represent minimal and highly conservative estimates of psychological impairment after a nuclear holocaust.

3

IMPLICATIONS OF DISASTER RESEARCH FOR CIVIL DEFENCE

Nuclear nations such as the US and the USSR officially endorse an evacuation policy, together with a degree of sheltering, though relatively little provision has been made in practice for all citizens. Some non-nuclear countries such as Switzerland have an official shelter policy, and have made extensive preparations for sheltering their citizens. Domestic housing must contain a reinforced shelter when a house is built, and hospitals and even factories have been constructed underground. Such precautions have some value when the expected threat is fallout from neighbouring countries, but offer less security in the case of direct nuclear attack.

Although the United Kingdom contains many nuclear and military targets, the present policy offers neither shelters nor evacuation. Although shelters exist for certain personnel, citizens are asked to remain at home. Economic and political considerations have prevented a shelter programme, and geographical constraints have restricted the scope for evacuation, though some parts of the country are likely to be safer than others (Openshaw, Steadman and Greene, 1983). Discussions on civil defence tend to proceed at two levels: public pronouncement, and confidential governmental preparation.

In the first category are most of the statements which governments issue for the guidance of the public. On the subject of nuclear war these are generally infrequent and muted. The subject is not normally raised in public pronouncements, and though official television announcements have given the public guidance on hazards such as domestic fires, none has been issued on the subject of nuclear attack. In this way the official avoidance of the topic parallels individual denial. Of the statements which have been made, the householder's booklet *Protect and Survive* (COI, 1980) is the best known. Originally intended for free distribution to all households, it was then simply offered for sale to the public.

In the second category is a series of confidential government documents and briefing papers, some of which have been informally communicated to journalists and researchers, and are in restricted circulation, occasionally reaching the public press. The planning documents behind civil defence exercises such as 'Square Leg' are in this category. An extensive study of these confidential preparations has been conducted by Campbell (1983).

Churcher and Lieven (1983) have noted the stress laid in these documents on the preservation of 'law and order', with less emphasis being placed on comforting the survivors. Survival is discussed without reference to psychological reactions, as it seems to be assumed that the main response to catastrophe is riot and insurrection.

Childs (1983) has attended civil defence courses for community volunteers (PAW, 1982), who are required to attend 12 evening meetings run by ex-forces officers. Although some technical information is imparted, the main emphasis of this essentially low-key approach is to shape attitudes. The theme of law and order dominates the discussions, and advisers are made to feel that they are part of a responsible, clear-headed minority who must control a panicky, self-interested public. In this way, Childs argues, potential community leaders are given a supposed survival role, and are deflected from reactions of horror or anger, and from participating in active prevention of the threat itself.

The general assumptions of civil defence have been severely criticized on scientific grounds (Openshaw, Steadman and Greene, 1983), medical grounds (BMA, 1983), and psychological grounds (Churcher *et al.*, 1981; Churcher and Lieven, 1983). A recent services defence studies symposium (Brassey's Publishers, 1982) presents a variety of views, and includes accounts of other nations' preparations.

Protect and Survive

No systematic studies of the comprehensibility and effects of this pamphlet have been reported. The prose style is simple, and the line drawings equally simple. The style is straightforward and unemotional, with the reassuring flavour of an official publication. It has changed little from the version circulated 20 years earlier, though some illustrations have been made more contemporary.

The first substantial message is that there is no way of knowing where the bombs will fall, and that radioactive fallout may be spread everywhere. Therefore no place is safer than any other, and the public should stay at home. They are encouraged to do so by the argument that their home is the place they know best, where they are known by their neighbours, and where they hold their food supplies. Additionally, there is the suggestion that abandoned homes could be expropriated for housing refugees.

The pamphlet then gives advice on the construction of an inner refuge – a makeshift construction of doors, tables and containers full of earth into which the family should go when the alert is sounded. Advice is given about gathering stores, which should include sufficient food for a fortnight. There is some further advice on waiting inside for the all-clear, and general hints on coping with living without mains services.

At times of nuclear crisis there would also be radio and television broadcasts and newspaper articles, but although pre-recorded tapes exist, they have not been made available publicly, so they cannot be evaluated psychologically.

Protect and Survive propagates several assumptions of civil defence planning for nuclear war which have been discussed by Churcher and Lieven (1983). First, it is assumed there will be warning and there will then be one attack from which people must then recover over something like a two-week period. It is assumed that food and supplies will be available to meet these demands. No mention is made of there being a series of attacks, or protracted nuclear war (Halloran, 1982). Second, it is assumed that the broadcasting services will survive destruction and that domestic receivers will survive electro-magnetic pulse, which is unlikely on technical grounds (Glasstone and Dolan, 1980). An injunction to keep aerials pushed in is the only oblique mention this phenomenon receives. The policy option of selectively disconnecting private subscribers from the telephone system in such an emergency (Campbell, 1983) is not mentioned, but if adopted, would severely increase psychological stress. Third, it is assumed that there will be an authority of some sort capable of giving guidance to survivors, though whether this will be civil or military is unclear. Fourth, it is assumed that householders are fit, healthy and capable of carrying out the instructions contained in the pamphlet. Problems of the elderly, infirm, or handicapped are not mentioned, nor the effects of discharging chronic patients from hospitals so as to prepare for casualties. Psychological reactions of anxiety and distress are not mentioned.

How will people react?

In the light of what is known about human reactions to disaster, and experimental studies of stress, what predictions can be made about the likely reactions to warning of nuclear war?

In the first place, no accurate predictions can be made without assuming that findings from other threats can be applied to nuclear warfare. This involves extrapolations about the extent of damage, and since this is likely to be very much worse than any disasters ever experienced, these will be minimal estimates.

Many factors are likely to determine the public response, and only the general tendencies can be outlined. Evidence from the previous chapter will be used in order to provide an informed speculation on likely reactions. Therefore the account that follows is an attempt to apply what is known from past catastrophes to a future event, and represents a best estimate given for illustrative purposes only.

The nature and timing of the warning

There is no guarantee that there will be any public warning of nuclear war.

Assuming that government organizations receive signals of imminent attack, there are several reasons for these not being made public. From the diplomatic point of view, the announcement of civil defence preparations could be viewed as a preparation for hostilities, and would contribute to increased political tension. As such, there would be considerable reluctance to make an official announcement. From the military point of view, the announcement of imminent war would disrupt civilian production and reduce the military's capacity to prepare for hostilities. Should the population begin to move out of urban centres the mobility of military units would be severely hampered, and this would be a strong reason for delaying public warnings.

From the domestic political point of view, warnings of nuclear war would carry immense political risks. They could be interpreted as an admission of the failure of policies of deterrence. If the crisis failed to materialize there would be inevitable political repercussions, and although any rational evaluation would suggest that this would be of little consequence for the nation, it might have considerable personal consequences for the decision maker. Katz (1982) has shown that major evacuation has profound economic consequences, with considerable social and industrial disruption. Titmuss (1950) has drawn attention to the highly damaging effects of the evacuation of British cities during the Second World War, which directly affected the daily lives of almost a third of the population. The government stripped the cities of their facilities and non-essential citizens, and transported them to rural areas which did not have the capacity to cope with them. When the expected immediate onslaught did not come, the government felt it had damaged its social services needlessly. It is possible that this painful experience has influenced official policy on evacuation to this day.

It is also likely that any announcement of nuclear threat would have a major motivating effect on anti-nuclear movements, and from the restricted vantage point of domestic politics, this could weigh heavily on decision makers.

For the above reasons, it cannot be guaranteed that warning signals will immediately be made public. Further, since nuclear war may begin by accident, the first warning may be the actual explosion.

Nuclear strike without warning

An unannounced nuclear explosion would be likely to cause massive and immediate stress responses and flight reactions in most of the population. Those at the outskirts of the explosion would undoubtably attempt to flee from the affected areas. A major determinant of this flight would be the extent of the subsequent fire, but a secondary cause would be fear of radiation. Most people whose houses remained relatively intact on the far outskirts of the explosion would be totally at a loss as to what they should do, and their behaviour may be determined by the alarm of witnessing injured and terrified fleeing survivors. There is likely to be mass fleeing, though for relatively short distances for most people. Depending on the state of the surrounding country, intact family groups will probably attempt to travel further, with no wish other than to distance themselves from the scene of the explosion. Those who have been separated from family members will mostly wish to return when major fires are over. They will probably do so despite radiation fears, and those who do not will be in a turmoil of indecision, tending to drift back unless forcibly prevented. None of these near-miss victims are likely to be capable of concerted rescue efforts, but will search in a disorganized fashion for missing family members while they are physically capable of doing so.

It is unlikely that official statements will have much influence on public behaviour at this stage. The failure to provide warning will be seen as a major dereliction of care. If the explosion is an isolated single accident then it is probable that public reactions could eventually be managed by massive media campaigns that stressed, however belatedly, practical tasks which would serve to reduce anxiety.

Unofficial warning

The most likely warning of nuclear hostilities will be as a culmination of news reports, unofficial preparations and 'leaks' about defence preparations. Whether a state of threat is thought to exist will depend on the individual's access to information and the interpretation which they place upon it. As in most other crises, some people will become alarmed quickly, while others will appear not to notice signs of danger. This condition is the most likely to generate a wide variety of individual reactions.

Some people will begin to make preparations, attempting to leave the country or moving to places of perceived relative safety.

Official warning

If an official warning is ever given, it may be a muted warning which stresses the purely precautionary nature of the exercise, or which describes the preparations as a form of fire-drill. Some time may then elapse before more specific and definite warnings are transmitted. In all the discussions which follow it is necessary to understand that different reactions are likely at different stages of the warning process. The warning will create a dilemma for many people, since they will have to balance their personal needs against those of the community (Killian, 1952). In terms of the social dilemmas reviewed by Dawes (1980), each individual will receive a higher payoff for a socially defecting choice, like hoarding food, but all individuals would benefit if they cooperated.

Reactions as warnings intensify

At the very early unofficial stages of warning those who have a vigilant coping style will begin preparing, though in a covert fashion. Holiday bookings abroad are likely to increase, food hoarding may begin and those who are unable to leave the country for supposed safety abroad may begin to search for places of greater perceived safety in the countryside.

Those who have a denying coping style will deny that danger exists, and will attempt to continue their lives as normally as possible, without any evacuation plans. Their ability to maintain denial will depend on the continued availability of food and services, particularly entertainment which makes no reference to nuclear matters.

In this state of tense ambiguity chance factors may play a large part. Other news may distract attention, or minor political developments may be seen as offering hope of an early solution to international political tensions. Extraneous factors such as fine weather may assist the denial process, and make the threat seem less believable to many people. Rumour may lead to public alarm, with food hoarding a likely starting point. Petrol may also be hoarded, since it will come to represent a necessity in any evacuation. Dawes (1980) points out that people must have some reason for believing that others will not defect from the social requirements if they are to follow the cooperative path, and that belief is unlikely to exist in a crisis.

Once the state of warning achieves some official status, roughly 75% of the population will immediately enter a state of barely controlled fear and excitement. There will be an immense upsurge in telephone calls to friends and relatives, followed by travelling as families try to unite. There will be continuous and obsessive monitoring of all news media. Should the government institute its plans for the selective disconnection of the private subscribers telephone system, immense anxiety will result. Any restrictions on private travel will further increase anxiety, and will be evaded wherever possible.

The clearing out of many patients from hospitals to make way for the injured will place many families under increased stress and practical difficulties.

At the same time it is possible that a small proportion of the population, say 5% to 10%, will continue to deny the threat, and will believe that 'the whole thing will blow over'.

Some of those who had originally been deniers will go into a state of extreme anxiety. This condition, which will also affect those who have always been anxious and vigilant, is likely to handicap roughly 15% of the population.

Rural and urban reactions

There will most probably be differences in the precautionary activities of urban and rural dwellers. Most people perceive urban centres as being prime targets, since they always were so during the Second World War. Although most military targets are not in urban centres, their locations are not readily known to the general public, and many rural locations are seen as safe even though in reality they contain probable targets. In a recent survey, Gunter and Wober (1982) report that 38% of Londoners said they would try to leave the city if there was a nuclear attack. This may prove to be a minimal estimate, and under threat the percentage may be substantially higher. The availability of food will be a major determinant of people's movements. Those who own second homes or who have relatives in rural locations will be likely to make for them as soon as they have stocked up on food. Urban dwellers without rural homes or relatives will either attempt to find friends or seek hotel accommodation. It is likely that their destination will be holiday locations and places they associate with rural calm. Depending on the speed with which the crisis develops people will either attempt to secure hotel bookings or will finally leave the cities in the hope of finding bed and breakfast accommodation. Even at this stage the threat may seem unreal, and people may wish to have cover stories to account for their flight from the cities. They will want to take their holidays early, and will make for areas which they associate with relaxation and unstressed living. People will be reassured by seeing open spaces, trees, farms and in general places which do not look like concentrated industrial and military targets. Rural dwellers foresee that urban evacuees will threaten their own chances of survival. Their main wish will be to protect themselves from the expected urban influx, and they may organize for that purpose. If rooms are offered to evacuees then country people may expect to be partly or entirely paid with food. Visitors without food supplies are unlikely to be offered shelter.

Perception of vulnerability will be crucial. Although many military targets are in rural areas, these will probably not be known to holiday visitors. Some people may unwittingly journey from the vicinity of secondary targets to major targets in the countryside. In general, however, the dispersal of the population to areas of low population density is a rational survival policy, since it would increase the numbers of immediate survivors. A fully dispersed population has a higher chance of survival than when clustered into urban centres. A mere 116 nuclear weapons directed at population centres could kill half the population outright. The bulk of the effect would be caused by the first 20 bombs (Openshaw, Steadman and Greene, 1983).

Will people stay at home?

Several factors will determine whether the majority of the population remains at home when the threat of nuclear attack is evident.
1. Urban dwellers are more likely to leave their homes than rural people.
2. The young are more likely to leave than the elderly.

3. In a situation where the threat is ambiguous, factors such as season, weather, shortages of food and essential supplies will play an important part.

Taking all factors together, and considering what is known of human reactions to disaster, it is highly unlikely that most people will stay in urban centres after an official warning of attack. It is far more likely that people will begin leaving once threat is evident and that any attempts to stop them will merely increase the flight from the cities.

Effects of sheltering

Once people have moved from areas of perceived danger, they are likely to attempt to construct some form of shelter, more as a form of anxiety reduction than because of any beliefs about the safety it will confer. A rough and ready arrangement within a house will be the most common construction. Whilst radio and television broadcasts continue they will probably remain within easy reach of this shelter, but are unlikely to stay in it except possibly for sleeping in it at night.

Whether people stay in their shelters after impact will depend on the extent of blast damage and the spread of fire. In moderately damaged houses people will probably attempt to flee. If fire threatens then this will be certain. In lightly damaged houses away from fire zones people are more likely to remain near their shelter, but most will leave the house for brief periods to see what has happened outside.

Although isolation in a shelter can cause stress and irritability to volunteers under normal circumstances, the more extreme effects of sensory isolation are unlikely to occur. Cleveland *et al.* (1963) found that a middle class family of four were able to undertake a two-week shelter confinement without deleterious effects other than increased irritability and depression. However, Beussee *et al.* (1970) admit that none of these volunteer studies can simulate the psychological stresses of real nuclear attack.

For those who are far from the effects of blast, once the exhilaration of immediate survival is over, the main stressors will be fear of radiation and grief for those who are dead. If physical injuries have occurred, as will probably be the case for most households which have sustained blast damage, then the aftermath will be traumatising. No medical facilities will be available, and stress will cause reactions indistinguishable from the early stages of radiation sickness. If further explosions are experienced during this time then anxiety levels will be intolerable.

Summary and conclusions

On the basis of what is known about human responses to disaster, as described in Chapter 2, and the official preparations for civil defence, described in this chapter, certain conclusions can be drawn about the most probable psychological effects of nuclear attack upon the United Kingdom.

The psychological consequences of a single nuclear explosion on an urban centre will so raise the level of psychological distress in both the immediate survivors and the surrounding people that the conventional resources will be overwhelmed. If no other part of the country is damaged then there will be a gradual return to quasi-normal functioning in the community but the survivors are likely to be permanently affected, and most will be severely impaired.

Five or six nuclear explosions on urban centres will so raise the level of psychological distress in survivors that the continued functioning of a recognizable social structure will be in question. A return to quasi-normal functioning is less likely, and it is more probable that there will be permanent and severe impairment, with a distortion and disintegration of the present social organization.

A nuclear attack on the United Kingdom at the expected level of roughly 200 megatons will leave the 15 million or so immediate survivors severely and permanently impaired, and will destroy their capacity for productive social interaction. Given the further consequences which will follow upon the destruction of the economy, the capacity of the survivors to reconstruct any form of functioning society without massive and sustained outside help will be negligible. It is highly unlikely that a civilized society will survive.

4

HUMAN FALLIBILITY AND NUCLEAR WEAPONS

A weapon is an enemy even to its owner. Turkish proverb.

No human enterprise can ever be infallible, though hope may make it seem so before the event. Being human, we all make mistakes, the impact of which will depend on their context. Arbours and Karrick (1951) define an accident as 'an unplanned event in a chain of planned or controlled events'. More succinctly, Cherns (1962) has called it 'an error with sad consequences'. While there is a large human involvement in the management, control and maintenance of nuclear weapon systems, it is inevitable that mistakes will happen.

Such mistakes are only admitted when they cannot be denied. Aeroplane accidents over populated zones have to be discussed fairly openly, while submarine collisions and computer malfunctions can be accorded less public attention. United States policy is to report nuclear weapons mishaps only if there is public alarm or danger to the public. Soviet Union policy is not to report accidents, therefore available reports on both countries come from US sources or independent bodies such as SIPRI.

The US Department of Defense has conceded that by 1981 there had already been 32 major accidents in US forces alone, and independent sources put the figure for both major and minor accidents at 113 by 1977 (SIPRI, 1981). Despite lack of reporting, 6 accidents and 16 incidents are known to have occurred to Warsaw Pact forces. Four incidents occurred to French forces, and 8 to United Kingdom forces. Because of lack of information the gravity of these events is not known.

Nuclear weapons themselves are reportedly able to withstand trauma without triggering a full nuclear explosion, though the possibility still exists (US Atomic Energy Commission and Department of Defense, 1962). However, each accident reveals new problems. In 1961 near

Goldsboro, North Carolina a B-52 bomber broke up in flight, releasing two 24-megaton bombs. Airforce experts found that on one of the bombs five of the six interconnecting safety devices had been set off by the fall, leaving only one to prevent an explosion. At least seven nuclear weapons have been jettisoned from aircraft, and at least three were never recovered. There have been 14 cases of radioactive contamination following nuclear accidents.

Most accidents have involved aircraft, but incidents have also occurred in nuclear submarines and missile silos. In September 1980 a technician working on a Titan II inter-continental ballistic missile dropped a socket wrench onto a fuel tank below. The tank lost fuel, and some hours later exploded, blasting open the silo's 740-ton door and shooting the 9-megaton warhead six hundred feet into the air. Frantic radio messages were overheard as the survivors tried to find the warhead. In 1980, 21 incidents had occurred at Titan missile silos, which were put down to inexperience of the operators, and ageing of the missiles (Defence Monitor, 1981).

Possibly even more serious are errors in signal detection. In November 1979, a war game training tape was accidentally fed into a NORAD computer, and was accepted as real, initiating a low level nuclear war alert as personnel prepared launch procedures (Beres, 1980). In June 1980, two false alarms were traced to computer malfunctions. False alarms are common, and the system depends on computers which have difficulty coping with the mass of data fed to them, and which rely on electronic chips which may be unreliable, though attempts are being made to improve the system (Borning, 1984).

Apart from technical errors, false alarms have also arisen as the result of practical jokes, hoax messages and accident. Dumas (1982) cites a reported case of a Minuteman crew who played a practical joke by recording a launch message and playing it when the next shift came to relieve them. It is quite feasible that such dangerous 'pranks' are one means of relieving the boredom and monotony of their working conditions. Further accounts of nuclear accidents can be found in SIPRI (1977), Defence Monitor (1981), Dumas (1982) and Britten (1983).

Isolated accidents arising from inadvertent departures from correct operating procedures are not the only problems which arise from nuclear weapons systems. A greater concern is that the system itself may have been mistakenly designed so that it cannot operate safely. For example, the carrying out of necessary additional defensive procedures during a high level alert may give the opposing side the mistaken impression that it is about to be attacked (Bracken, 1983).

Section 1. **Approaches to risk assessment**

Risk assessment is a growing field, and many publications have appeared in recent years, reflecting growing concern with safety estimation (Dowie and Lefrere, 1980; Green, 1982; Royal Society, 1983).

Britten (1983) has identified three main approaches to the assessment of risk. The most usual approach is the historical method, in which the number of accidents per unit time is recorded. This has some validity when the events are reasonably frequent, but is almost useless when assessing the risk of an event which has never occurred. Further, it must be pointed out that the fact that an event has not yet occurred does not of itself logically affect future risk. A long accident-free period may be reassuring, but one cannot, for example, argue that because one has lived for many years one is immortal.

Fault tree analysis is another common approach. This is the study of individual component failure rates, and their further effects upon larger systems of which they are part. The aim is to build in safety mechanisms in series, and make important errors unlikely. In theory, if a particular component has a one in ten chance of failure, then by fitting two into a system the chance of failure can be reduced to the product of the individual reliabilities, in this case one in a hundred. In practice it is never possible to rule out common mode failures, in which all individual components are affected. For example, at Brown's Ferry nuclear power plant, one of the largest in the world, an operator, breaking all safety rules, tried to find the source of an air leak in a tunnel by lighting a candle. In the resultant fire of insulating material, as operators struggled to retain control of the plant, it was belatedly realized that all cables to the supposedly independent safety systems went through this one tunnel (Comey, 1975).

An additional problem of a psychological nature is that one can never be sure that the official fault tree covers all eventualities. People tend to accept that the presented fault tree covers all events. Fischoff, Slovic and Lichtenstein (1978) found that people were quite insensitive to how much had been left out of a fault tree for a well-known problem – a car's failure to start. Deleting branches responsible for about half of all car starting failures only produced a 7% increase in people's estimates of what was missing. Car mechanics were about as insensitive as other subjects, suggesting that what was out of sight was out of mind. Fault trees may therefore be incomplete (the car start example omitted vandalism, a typical oversight) or may pay too much attention to minor matters by providing separate fault branches. Such an arrangement could exaggerate the number of apparent fault lines in which errors were unlikely. Vandalism, terrorism and irrational personnel rarely figure in fault trees.

In summary, decisions about categorization can have major effects on the perception of risks, and although fault trees assist in understanding the effects of component failure, they cannot fully cover or assess all operating risks.

The last common approach to risk assessment is human factors analysis, which is the attempt to measure the error rates of human operators under different circumstances. This work arises from ergonomics, the science of fitting machines to the capabilities and limitations of their operators. As Britten (1983) points out, it can be argued that all system failures result from human error, whether in design, production, maintenance or operation. Attempts to chain together task error rates into a human fault tree are limited and potentially misleading. These approaches assume that an error in one task makes it no more likely that there will be an error in a subsequent task. Yet all the psychological evidence would suggest that this is untrue (Meister, 1977). Individuals are not only affected by their own errors, they are also prone to the 'common mode failures' of feeling bored, anxious, resentful and sometimes downright malevolent. A fuller view of man is needed if we are to begin to understand errors and accidents.

Section 2. **Decision-making, and the prospects for rationality**

There is little argument that when people are inebriated, under stress or in a very great hurry they can make serious errors of judgement. However, even sober, calm subjects, given time and adequate facilities are subject to considerable limitations in their rational thinking. This signifies that human beings cannot compute all the outcomes required from theories of rational choice, and have to resort to intuitive methods (Simon, 1983).

When it is necessary to make a decision in a complex and uncertain situation, people tend to be unable to fully work out all the statistical probabilities, and fall back on rules of thumb. These intuitions tend to be biased in ways which people do not realize, even when they are trying hard to make rational decisions. Superficial features of the problem may distort judgements, and such errors are only revealed by the more rigorous and time consuming methods of statistical analysis.

These shortcomings have been the subject of intensive study, and the work of Tversky and Kahneman (1974) has had a major impact. Some of the implications of this fascinating field are reviewed in Kahneman, Slovic and Tversky (1982) and only a few of the main points relevant to the nuclear case can be mentioned here.

The main shortcomings of intuitive judgements can be categorized as misconceptions about representativeness and limitations on the availability of instances.

(i) Representativeness

People tend to be insensitive to base rates. Even when they are told that one condition is more frequent than another they tend to be unduly influenced by stereotypes. For example, when given a description of a person as introverted and shy, and asked whether such a person is more likely to be a librarian or a farmer, most judge the person described to be a librarian. However, since there are many more farmers than librarians, on a probability basis the person is more likely to be a farmer. It would appear that personality information has more impact than any knowledge about base rates.

This insensitivity to base rates has considerable practical consequences when it comes to making decisions on the basis of imperfect detection techniques. Consider as an example the situation in which a decision must be made about whether to operate on a patient, given a particular result from a medical test.

The decision cannot rationally be made on the test results alone, since all tests have false positive and false negative detection errors. That is to say, some patients who have the disease are mistakenly classified as healthy, and some healthy patients falsely identified as being ill. When the false positive rates are relatively high and the prevalence of the disease is relatively low, many people may be mistakenly identified as needing an operation. It is very clear that doctors are generally unable to deal with these probabilities intuitively (Casscells, Schoenberger and Graboys, 1978; Eddy, 1982), with considerable consequences when detecting conditions such as breast cancer. The implications for the nuclear case are disturbing, since it would appear that subjects are likely to evaluate attack warnings in an intuitive fashion without adequate reference to prior probabilities. These are hard to calculate in the nuclear case, but appear to be derived from assessments of the likely pattern of troop and weapons movements prior to an attack (Bracken, 1983).

Since nuclear decision-makers must continually be on guard against misinterpreting chance events, subjective estimates about chance are of particular interest. It would appear (Tversky and Kahneman, 1971) that even highly trained researchers have a lingering belief in the 'law of small numbers' and place too much trust in the representativeness of small samples. A short run of chance events could be overinterpreted, particularly because people assume that even in a short run of outcomes there will be a miniature representation of the overall laws of chance. For example, people tend to imagine that in six throws of a coin the number of heads and tails should be equal, and that there should not be a long run of heads or tails.

> Chance is commonly viewed as a self correcting process in which a deviation in one direction induces a deviation in the opposite direction to restore the equilibrium. In fact, deviations are not corrected as a chance process unfolds, they are merely diluted. (Tversky and Kahneman, 1974, p.1125)

(ii) Availability

When trying to look ahead to the consequences of a decision, there are biases as to what can be imagined and what is available to be retrieved from memory. This affects risk perception and the capacity to design adequate fault trees.

Illusory correlation is a phenomenon in which the salience of a few chance events misleads people into judging that they always go together.

A final well-known and very powerful bias is the emotional impact of the individual case. As Russell (1927) observed, 'popular induction depends upon the emotional interest of the instances, not upon their number'. *In vivo* face to face instances have more power than large number statistics, and a particularly dramatic event may have an impact out of all proportion to the small addition it makes to sample size. As Simon (1983) points out, emotion may serve as a way of focusing our attention on the fact that a choice needs to be made, but it can severely affect our judgement. Intuitive rationality, in his view, depends on extensive practice, and even in a highly trained practitioner is still subject to the many biases described above, most of them the more pernicious by being unknown to the subjects.

All these findings make it clear that in high risk technologies where speedy decisions are required even well-motivated and trained subjects can make serious errors of judgement by relying on intuition.

Section 3. **The psychology of accidents**

Skilled behaviour requires that a planned sequence of rehearsed behaviours be organized into a particular sequence in order to obtain a desired consequence. At every stage checks must be carried out in order to ensure that it is appropriate to carry on to the next stage of the task. Each rehearsed sequence may have different levels of competence, brought about by different amounts of practice. Some skills will be so familiar that they can be carried out without conscious attention, and will be reverted to at times of stress or inattention. Some will have been learned in particular contexts which are now no longer relevant to the task in question. At each choice point in the sequence of tasks it is necessary to remember where one is in the planned sequence, and to evaluate the need to continue. At any point events may occur which should lead to the abandonment of the original plan, and the adoption of entirely new emergency plans. The force of habit which helps sustain the skilled execution of the original plan may prevent a flexible response when new circumstances arise.

Problems can arise when a slip or lapse occurs in a well planned sequence, leading to an execution failure. Equally important, a mistake may be made in planning, so that incorrect choices may be made. Such planning failures are more complex, subtle and potentially more dangerous. Rules of thumb may be used inappropriately, leading to mistaken judgements (Kahneman, Slovic and Tversky, 1982).

A large number of factors can affect performance. In addition to stress produced by the demands of the task in hand, individuals also have to deal with other environmental information, such as noise, illumination and temperature. These will, in turn, interact with their cognitive appraisal of the situation, and their subjective mood, which of itself can be an important factor in performance. The subjective state can be modified on a transient basis by the ingestion of psychoactive drugs and alcohol, which also have direct effects on task performance (Hindmarch, 1980). More long term and continuous effects, e.g. mood changes, feelings of boredom, restlessness and irritability can be induced by conditions of reduced environmental stimulation, such as social and perceptual deprivation (Kubzansky, 1961; Taylor *et al.*, 1968). Such conditions are of particular relevance to those military personnel involved in nuclear weapons control, given the increased reliance on automated equipment, which is monitored either in the restricted environment of a submarine, or an isolated nuclear station.

The following are some of the major factors which affect individual skilled behaviour.

(i) Attentional factors

Dixon (1983) has identified the problem of 'attention narrowing', which is a frequent cause of accidents. Operators become engrossed with minor problems, and develop a tunnel vision in which vital pieces of information may be ignored, leading to major problems. For example, a flight crew attempting to understand why the light confirming the lowering of the undercarriage had not come on failed to note that they had accidently disengaged the autopilot and were losing height. They continued to solve the indicator light problem, to establish whether the wheels had safely locked down, and did not note the larger problem, the disengagement of the autopilot, until the very moment when the plane flew into the ground (Dixon, 1983).

(ii) Perceptual distortion

Reason (1982) has studied accidents as examples of catastrophic lapses of concentration in skilled behaviour, and has identified component features of such events.

The first is due to errors in the human links of a communication chain. One pervasive bias is the tendency for messages to become distorted in the direction of expected inputs, not the faithful rendering of actual inputs (Campbell, 1958). If the message has become distorted with 'noise' of some sort, which makes it more difficult to discriminate and more ambiguous, then people are most likely to pass on something which fits their preconceptions. When the expected input fits in with the messenger's attitude and desires this bias is intensified.

Perceptual distortion can occur when stimuli are ambiguous, when past experience and training lead to inappropriate interpretations, and when strong emotions shift perception in the direction of wish-fulfilling fantasies. In military settings there is the additional bias of not passing on information which may lead to disciplinary proceedings.

The second source of error is that human renderings of messages tend to be far shorter than the originals, which results in abbreviation, simplification and loss of detail.

These features, heavily implicated in the classic military disaster, the Charge of the Light Brigade, contribute errors to all communication systems which involve human interpretation and transmission.

(iii) Cognitive set

A third source of error is the human preference for confirming rather than disconfirming evidence. Given a mistaken hypothesis, people are more willing to search vainly for confirmation than to test it destructively, and abandon it the moment it is found wanting. A hypothesis remains a personal interpretation and view of reality, and people cling to them rather than face confusion and the strain of reconstructing their mental attitudes (Wason, 1964). This means that even in conditions of obvious danger attempts will be made to persist with incorrect interpretations of orders, and when this is coupled with military obedience to orders, tragedies can result, such as the sinking of HMS Victoria as a result of a collision arising from ambiguous and misinterpreted naval orders (Reason, 1982). Watkins (1970) has named this the imperfect rationality principle, whereby one does not dismiss apparently irrational acts as moments of madness, but attempts to understand them as imperfect attempts to make sense of a problem. It must be noted that once an imperfect understanding has taken root, then it is very hard to dislodge that interpretative framework, and facts which call it into question may be discredited, reinterpreted or ignored.

(iv) Vigilance

Military researchers have long had an interest in the factors which make for efficient watchkeeping. Time of day shows an association with reaction time, frequency of errors in industrial work and even falling asleep while driving (Hildebrandt, 1974). Circadian rhythms are associated with fluctuations in alertness, and the watchkeeping patterns used in naval work do not always allow maximal adjustment. Colquhoun (1975) points to a considerable body of evidence confirming that time of day or night affects the capacity to notice faint signals of the sort commonly sought in military operations. In a study of prolonged undersea voyages Colquhoun *et al.* (1978) found important differences according to patterns of watchkeeping. Where duties must be commenced immediately after journeys across time zones, as occurs with commercial shipping crews, airline pilots and rapid response military units, the effects of desynchronized biological rhythms can be particularly disruptive. Although these factors are now given formal recognition in many settings, such as civil aviation, operating procedures do not always permit the best arrangements in practice. Further accounts can be found in Colquhoun (1971).

(v) Motivational factors

Motivational factors are a major component in performance. They determine which jobs get done and how they get done. They may also determine whether ventures can be initiated at all, and may effectively determine which aspects of a programme can actually be completed. In peacetime conditions motivation is generally low, and the general level of performance may suffer as a consequence. The Falklands war showed that an emergency can generate so much higher a level of motivation that repair work, industrial work and the provision of ships can be carried out much faster than in peace time. In describing this as an emergency it may be incorrectly assumed that this is an exceptional state which has no further consequences for everyday productivity. What these major social effects make evident is that motivational changes properly harnessed are several orders of magnitude greater than any other effects in training personnel. These major effects remain difficult to study, since they cannot be properly simulated. Every account of preparation for combat underlines the finding that real emergencies create a sense of urgency and importance that even the most realistic exercises lack. Although an emergency has a motivating effect, it also exacts a heavy cost, and even well-trained operators may find their performance disrupted when faced with real events (Thompson, 1983).

(vi) Anxiety, arousal and performance

The general curvilinear relationship between anxiety and performance is well known, and indicates that performance is best within moderate levels of arousal. Too low a level of arousal will cause careless and inattentive performance. Too high a level will cause overactive and excitable behaviour, with frequent errors. For people who must carry out repetitive vigilance tasks the main determinant of arousal is the level of stimulation. Low rates of stimulation lead to boredom and poor performance. Dumas (1982) has drawn attention to the endless hours spent by nuclear service personnel interacting with computer consoles, isolated from other human beings, endlessly practising routines which they are never allowed to complete. Boredom and social isolation are compounded by secrecy, which prevents them from discussing their work. Finally, anxiety will be aroused in most subjects by the potential consequences of their actions, and although these thoughts may be suppressed they will contribute to the perceived stressfulness of the job. Although an anxious and aroused crew may perform better if they have been well trained in their duties, the stress of long-term maintenance of arousal is likely to affect a sizeable proportion of even well-selected and well-trained personnel, resulting in both a decrease in performance and a less predictable performance.

(vii) Social isolation and social stress

Most service lives show disruption because of two main effects. Firstly, separation of entire families from a suitable broad based community, and secondly, separation of one family member from the family while on extended duty. It is not uncommon to find higher than usual levels of psychological distress in service families, with problems which tend to focus on fears about the viability of the home, fidelity of spouses, and difficulties inherent in bringing up children, who are subject to frequent moves and absences of the parent. From a clinical point of view, factors can be divided into the extrinsic and the intrinsic. Extrinsic factors are: frequent moves in the community, separation of family, inability to plan sensibly in the long term, and discontinous career with early retirement, all of which tend to disrupt psychological adjustment. Such extrinsic factors encourage quickly made and quickly forgotten friendships outside the service, and foster stronger links within the services. Intrinsic factors are: recruits are attracted by the family aspects of the total institution; service life reduces the uncertainty of civilian living, by offering an organized structure with rewards and punishments which can reduce the pressure of personal responsibility. Such people can be good obeyers and poor initiators, who rely on an intact command structure, and may fail to point out mistaken decisions by their superiors (Thompson, 1983).

(viii) Drug abuse

Some of the above factors can lead service personnel to abuse drugs. Alcohol is the most abused drug in our culture and to some extent can be tolerated since some of its immediate and short-term effects are known and the symptoms of intoxication can generally be recognized. The Royal Air Force rule 'twelve hours from bottle to throttle' indicates the pragmatic approach to this problem. However, drugs may have less well-known effects, and hallucinogenic drugs offer the disturbing prospect of relapses occurring under stress. The figures for drug abuse amongst the military are not readily available, though the Freedom of Information Act in the USA has led to some disclosures. It would be wrong to think that the American problem is necessarily worse than those of other nuclear powers, and in the absence of other data American figures will continue to be taken as a first approximation.

The findings of two large surveys to investigate the extent of drug and alcohol abuse in the American services were presented to the US congress in 1981. The larger survey (Burt, 1980) was carried out through questionnaires administered to 16,355 active duty personnel throughout 81 locations world wide, of which 15,268 were returned completed, a response rate of 93%. Nonmedical drug use was highest in the unmarried, male, young enlisted groups and also correlated with lower educational attainment. Alcohol abuse affected all grades and in particular the higher grades, while other drugs mainly affected lower grades. Despite selection into the forces, overall drug usage for service personnel is at about the same level as unselected young civilians, suggesting that recruiters may be making up quotas without setting sufficiently high standards. The following table compiled from this survey (Congressional Record, 1981) shows overall levels of drug usage for US Department of Defense Personnel. Figures for younger enlisted personnel are shown separately because this is such a large group within the services, as compared to their lower representation in the population as a whole. They comprise 10,154 of the total survey sample.

Table 1. DoD Population using each drug in 1980 survey (percentages)

Drug type	Total DoD		18–25-year-olds	
	Past 30 days	Past 12 months	Past 30 days	Past 12 months
Marijuana/hashish	26	35	37	49
Amphetamines/uppers	6	13	9	19
Cocaine	4	11	7	17
Hallucinogens	3	8	5	12
Tranquilizers	2	6	3	8
Barbiturates/downers	2	6	3	8
Opiates	1	4	2	5
PCP	1	4	1	6
Heroin	1	2	1	2
Any drug use	27	36	38	50
Alcohol	83	n/a	84	93

From this table it will be noted that drugs which might be expected to maximally impair performance, and possibly render the user vulnerable, are used in an uncomfortably high percentage, especially for the younger men. The survey also found that the greatest problem was that of poly-drug abuse, in which men mixed alcohol and/or other drugs. This had led to deaths and serious illness.

Some effects of this level of drug usage can be gained from the following table from the same survey.

Table 2. Work impairment because of drug use (percentage of 18 to 25-year-olds)

Type of impairment	Total
Lowered performance	10
Late for work/left early	6
Did not come to work	4
High while working	19
Total: any impairment	21

The service breakdown indicated that, apart from the Air Force at 8%, about a quarter of the personnel in other services admitted being high while at work. As an example of some of the effects of drug abuse, on June 18th that year a marine EA-6B aircraft crashed on the deck of the USS Nimitz. An autopsy performed on the 14 marines and sailors killed revealed that six had recently taken drugs.

Results were also presented from a questionnaire survey of 1906 personnel in Italy and West Germany carried out in 1981 for the Select Committee on Narcotics and Drug Abuse under the leadership of Congressman English. This survey found even higher levels of drug use.

The figures on this survey for the US Navy indicated 49% on duty admitted drug usage, mostly cannabis, but including hard drugs. Many servicemen are poly-drug abusers, and even seriously incapacitated addicts may remain in highly sensitive posts for long periods, due to staff shortages, before action is taken (Dumas, 1980). It has also been reported that there is some difficulty in attracting and keeping nuclear personnel (Observer, 1981).

The following table is taken from the Select Committee's investigation of military drug abuse.

Table 3. Question: 'During the last month, have you used any of the following while on duty (during working hours)?' (Percentages indicate affirmative answers)

	Army	Air Force	Marines	Navy
Marijuana/Hashish	38.00%	4.50%	24.34%	41.86%
Cocaine	3.03%	0	3.90%	3.82%
Heroin	1.99%	0	0.55%	0.57%
Uppers	9.60%	0	13.70%	27.05%
Downers	4.56%	0	4.90%	10.13%
LSD and other drugs	2.58%	0	2.20%	8.84%
Alcohol	28.01%	15.70%	19.40%	20.95%

Commenting on the results of these surveys, General Louissell admitted to the hearing:

> We have looked at the consequences of substance abuse in the armed forces. The results are not reassuring: 7% of the armed forces reported they were alcohol dependent; 4% reported themselves drug dependent. This can be dramatised by saying that there are at least 130,000 members of the armed forces who were substance dependent last year! Nine% of the E1–E5 population, (18–25 year olds) reported they were high on drugs at work at least 40 times in a year; 2% of all servicemen reported they were high/drunk on alcohol at work 40 times or more in a year. This percentage can be translated to say that there were at least 170,000 soldiers, sailors, marines and airmen on the firing ranges, in the manoeuvre areas, on the decks and in the maintenance shops, who were high or drunk 40 or more times last year!

He went on to report that one in five servicemen reported lower performance on duty due to alcohol abuse.

At the time of writing only summarized highlights of the 1982 Congressional investigations were available. These indicate some improvement in levels of drug use, but alcohol abuse has increased by 10%, possibly as a compensation for the attempted crack-down on drugs (Bray *et al.*, 1983).

These levels of drug abuse extend to US personnel based in the United Kingdom, where 455 drugs charges were preferred in the last year (*The Times*, 1984). Although this included troops on nuclear duties, this number was said to be 'totally insignificant'.

Despite requests, it has not been possible to obtain data on the full extent of the problem for British service personnel. In a written reply in Parliament (*Hansard*, 1984) 73 cases of drug abuse were admitted for 1983, but no data have been given on alcohol abuse, which is likely to be the largest category. Nothing has been made available about British selection procedures.

No data are available on Russian selection procedures, though independent sources point to extensive alcohol abuse in the general population (Feshbach, 1982).

Nuclear weapons personnel. These high rates of drug abuse in conventional military settings make accidents more likely, but even more serious consequences would result if such abuse extends to those who carry out nuclear weapons duties. About 120,000 service personnel are involved in US nuclear weapon duties. Their tasks include maintenance, guarding, transporting, training, and ultimately using the weapons. Such men are initially screened through a Personnel Reliability Program. In spite of this screening Congress heard (*Congressional Record*, 1978) that approximately 5000 people are removed annually from nuclear weapons duties.

This would suggest that either the screening is very poor, or the nature of the work is so stressful that many vulnerable servicemen may fall into drug abuse or criminal activities as a result. In fact, both are probably true. Reports on the Personnel Reliability Program, elsewhere in the congressional records, show it is not the thorough screening that would be required to select only the most suitable people for this exacting work.

> We have identified those duty positions where the incumbent requires certification and have established procedures to ensure individuals in those positions meet certain reliability standards. Before an individual is assigned to a PRP position he or she is carefully screened. The personnel record, including any unfavourable information is reviewed. Medical records are also reviewed and

if necessary a medical interview is conducted. The immediate commander then interviews the member and based on all available information, decides whether or not the individual is acceptable. If not acceptable the individual is disqualified. (*present author's emphasis*)

From this it does not seem that the individuals are necessarily seen by a doctor or psychologist who could judge if drugs or mental instability were going to be important in the individual case. The present procedure would seem to result in large numbers of unreliable people working in contact with nuclear weapons for varying periods before they are identified. Additionally, the sensitivity of the PRP is not known. It may be leaving in larger numbers of unreliable service personnel than it excludes. Without independent measures this cannot be evaluated.

Incidents involving US servicemen working with nuclear weapons whilst 'high' in this country have already emerged. In December 1981, documents were found on a rubbish tip by a local resident near to the base at Holy Loch. A nuclear weapons guard had marijuana on board, and had repeatedly failed to turn up for official duties, while a fireman on the USS Holland mother ship was using and trading in LSD, cocaine

Table 4. Removals from nuclear weapons duties

Reason	1975	1976	1977	1980*
Alcohol abuse	169	184	256	599
Drug abuse	1970	1474	1365	1726
Negligence or delinquency in performance of duty	703	737	828	
Court martial or civil convictions	345	388	350	
Behaviour or actions contemptuous of the law	722	945	885	
Significant physical, mental, or character trait or aberrant behaviour, medically substantiated as prejudicial to reliable performance	1219	1238	1289	
Total	5128	4966	4973	5324

*1980 figures added where available (*Congressional Record, 1981*)

and amphetamines. The court-martial papers giving full details of both cases have been seen by the author.

In view of the figures on 'on-duty' drug abuse quoted earlier, these incidents are hardly surprising and may represent an under-estimate of the problem.

It is known that alcohol and drug abuse depress performance, and may send people to sleep on duty. In the case of hallucinogenic drugs, mood changes, loss of contact with reality and even psychotic processes may be triggered. In this latter case even if the drugs are not used on duty they may impair subsequent performance.

(ix) The ultimate nature of the work

Most training for war prepares servicemen to fight other servicemen. Nuclear duties impose a major stress in that they involve the different task of threatening civilian populations. This emotional burden cannot lightly be dismissed, though it will not affect all people equally. Few accounts are available in the open literature as to how much of a stress this imposes on nuclear weapons operators. Wye (1971) an American missile operator writing under a pseudonym, observes:

> A crew member tries not to think about his ultimate responsibility, which could lead to the killing of millions of people...He is not supposed to have a conscience...He learns to contrast his personal feeling and the role he is expected to play unquestioningly and automatically. The hypocrisy of this game he's playing creates a feeling of disinvolvement. He tends to see his personal life and official life as totally separate: the launch officer becomes shizoid.

Nuclear duties impose a cognitive dissonance between the inherent morality of being a good person and the untenable immorality of large scale destruction. In order to resolve this dilemma most people attempt to preserve the status of their inherent morality, so the most common resolution is to deny the consequences of their behaviour. The major cognitive technique seems to be a predictive unreality, 'it may never come to that' or better still, 'because we do all this, it will never come to that'. The projection of evil intentions on to the other side is a useful option, and hidden within these mental adjustments is the belief that, after the event, none of the usual rules of morality need apply. Because nuclear duties may ultimately lead to participation in mass killing, special training techniques are used to diffuse personal responsibility and blunt emotional and moral reactions. Crew members are never told their targets, and repeatedly practise routines in which no one person can feel solely responsible for the actions taken. Even the language used in these settings is aimed to reduce the sense of personal responsibility. Crews do not 'fire' missiles, they 'enable' launch procedures.

It is difficult to estimate what proportion of nuclear crews will obey the order to fire, but from what is known of obedience to authority (Milgram, 1974) it is probable that the majority will do so. Only a very substantial change in attitudes leading to a sense of personal responsibility and empathy with the victims could disrupt the final performance of these destructive actions.

Section 4. Accident case histories

Accidents in civilian life are more open to public inspection than are those in military and nuclear areas. They are of particular interest when they occur in ways which had previously been considered highly unlikely, and where extensive and adequate safety precautions had been in force. They expose the myth of infallibility which grows up whenever a short-term gain in safety is made, or accidents have not occurred for some time, and reveal the new steps which must be taken to ensure safety in the future.

Perrow (1984) has made a major study of accidents in high-risk technologies, and his contribution has been to study the accident as a normal aspect of complex technological systems. He argues that the over-utilized concept of operator error restricts our understanding of the way complex systems operate, and his graphic accounts of mishaps in petro-chemical plants, nuclear power stations, transport systems and the like always stress the everyday production pressures under which people must normally operate. By the arresting term 'normal accident' Perrow focuses attention upon systems in which multiple failures which are not in direct operational sequence lead to unexpected interactions which result in an inevitable 'normal' accident.

Taking Three Mile Island as an example, Perrow rejects human error, mechanical failure, design and procedures as the primary cause of the accident, and puts the blame on the complexity of the system. Each of the failures, he argues, was trivial by itself, but since the entire system is 'tightly coupled', complex interactions occurred which were incomprehensible for a critical period. This is a common feature of system accidents, because the interactions generally cannot be seen, and often because they cannot be believed by the operators. In psychological terms, we often have to believe before we can see. Unwillingness to believe makes operators reject instrument readings, and persist with mistaken hypotheses, often making matters worse. Perrow makes the important point that unless they were able to behave in this fashion the plant could not operate, for otherwise every single untoward event would lead to a shutdown.

As a measure of the complexity of the tighly coupled nuclear power plant at Three Mile Island, Perrow notes that the major operator error (as determined by subsequent investigations) occurred just 13 seconds after the sudden rise in temperature which announced the crisis. No study of individual cognitive processes would do justice to explaining the highly complex system of which the operator was but one part.

Since all the systems to be discussed involve quality inspection and fault detection, the assumptions made about the efficiency of inspectors is an important issue. Smith (1981) has argued that the detection rates of quality inspectors searching for a rare fault in a supposedly safe system may be very much lower than some of the theoretical estimates which assume an inspector working at full capacity. This is because inspectors expend less effort when they believe that faults are unlikely, and when they imagine that anything of importance would have been found by another previous inspector. Smith argues that detection efficiencies should be based on empirical data wherever possible, and where none exist then conservative estimates, which take these points into account, should be used. In Smith's view these deficiencies account for the many faults experienced by systems which, on theoretical 'probability' grounds, should never have occurred.

Moorgate train crash

The Moorgate train crash of 28 February 1975 is important because it occurred in an underground train system with a good safety record and extensive safety systems, and because no system failures were found to explain the crash.

At 8.46 am the train driver drove his six-car train at between 30 and 40 mph through platform 9 and into the end wall of an overrun tunnel. Forty-two passengers and the driver were killed, and a further 72 injured, the worst accident in London Transport's history. On investigation all systems were found to have functioned perfectly, and the driver seemed to have kept the power on until almost the moment of impact. No evidence of drugs, illness, psychological problems or suicidal intent was found. He appeared to be his usual self that morning, and when he drove in the train on his third journey of the day, witnesses on the platform saw him seated at the controls looking perfectly normal. Reason (1982) feels that suicide or mental aberration were unlikely, on the basis of other evidence, and finds that a more probable explanation lies in 'imperfect rationality'. Reason argues that the driver may have suffered a mental lapse in which he 'lost his place' in the sequence of stations and imagined himself to be still one station away from the end of the line. Supportive evidence for this speculation is the fact that the lights in the approach tunnel to Moorgate were fully lit on the first two journeys but had been switched off on the last fatal journey, making the tunnel appear like all the other dark tunnels further up the line. If the driver had placed undue reliance on the lit tunnel as a visual cue that he was coming to the end of the line, then the absence of the lights could have been enough to confirm him in the false hypothesis that he still had one further station to go. When finally faced with clear evidence that he was coming in to the final station, the horrifying realization left him unable to react for the 10 seconds which separated him from disaster. It will now never be possible to know for sure what caused this crash, but the possibility of an attentional lapse compounded by a mistaken interpretative hypothesis being the most likely cause remains very strong. This was a case in which, despite many safety systems and many thousands of safe journeys over many years, human error caused a fatal accident. Long accident-free periods do not in themselves constitute proof that the possibility of error has been eliminated.

Tenerife runway collision

Another civilian accident which illuminates the chain of events whereby errors culminate in unfortunate consequences is the Tenerife runway collision of 27 March 1977. Despite all the efforts which have been expended in safety procedures, 577 people died in the collision, the worst in aviation history.

The causes of the disaster were multiple and complex, but reveal that errors occur when a cascade of events, each improbable and coincidental, leads to a final accident. A terrorist bomb had closed the main airport, and air traffic was diverted to the secondary airport of Santa Cruz, which quickly became congested, putting the three air traffic controllers under additional stresses. They had to devise impromptu taxi routes for the jets so that they could use the single fogbound runway, but had no ground radar to monitor their movements, and could only communicate on one radio frequency, since the other two had been out of action for six months. The flight crews had experienced long hours of duty, irritating delays, the prospect of further delays, and in the case of the KLM crew were approaching the legal limit of duty hours.

Two crucial errors led to the crash. The taxiing Pan Am flight did not turn off the runway at the indicated third taxiway, and the KLM flight took off before it had received final clearance to do so. The Pan Am flight may have missed the turning, or preferred to wait for the fourth turning which was more suitable for a jumbo jet. The KLM pilot appeared to be impatient to take off, and eventually did so on the basis of airway clearance, the stage before takeoff clearance. A possible explanation of this lapse in an exceptional pilot is that his extensive experience in training young pilots in simulators, in which 'flying time' had to be maximized at the cost of abbreviating the time-consuming radio procedures, had contributed fatally to his overriding of correct procedure. Over-exposure to simulated conditions, which can never totally reproduce real life events, may lead to short-cuts being mistakenly carried over to real situations.

Three Mile Island

At 4 am on 28 March 1979 there was a loss of coolant accident at the Three Mile Island unit 2 nuclear power plant. In the worst accident to occur in the history of the nuclear industry to date, the core of the reactor was partially uncovered and considerable damage to the plant occurred. A Presidential Commission (1979) reported on the accident and Canter and Powell (1983) have drawn out some of the psychological implications.

The Commission found that the accident occurred as a result of a series of human, institutional and mechanical failures. Equipment failures initiated the accident, but poor training, bad decisions, and a failure to understand what was happening made matters worse. Staff took too long to realize that core damage had occurred, and the design of the control room was deficient for dealing with emergencies. Over a hundred alarms sounded, and there was no way to switch off the unimportant ones so as to concentrate on essential warnings. During the first eight minutes of the accident operators did not realize that the emergency feedwater valve was closed because one of the indicator lights was covered with maintainance tags. Some key indicators were out of sight on the back of the control panel, some instruments went off-scale and remained so, and the computer printer registering alarms was running two and a half hours late, and at one point jammed, imposing further delays.

Canter and Powell (1983) draw attention to the fact that there was a total disregard for human–machine interaction in the design of the control room. The information needed by the operators was often non-existent, or poorly located, ambiguous or difficult to read. The control room had 1900 displays, of which 26% could not be seen when standing at the front panel. It was a classic example of information overload. Emergency procedures were not user-orientated, and although there were up to 30 operatives in the control room during the crisis, most of them did not understand what was happening to the plant. When interviewed by the Commission, operatives reported that what they most needed during the emergency was 'some way of knowing what was going on in the plant'. In psychological terms they were being subjected to 'noise' when what they needed were reliable signals. The prevailing atmosphere was one of total confusion, in which there was a lack of communication at all levels, and key decisions were taken without accurate information.

What the accident at Three Mile Island made plain was that complex systems require elaborate and effective information processing techniques for safe operation, and that the staff must be repeatedly trained in emergency procedures and must operate in control rooms which are based on an understanding of human factors in skilled performance. One damaging factor at TMI was the belief that nuclear energy was intrinsically safe, which led management and operators to ignore the possibility of serious malfunction. Although the industry had publicized reassuring risk estimates prior to this accident, such reassurance was partly responsible for the slack emergency training procedures. The President's Commission concluded:

> In conclusion, while the major factor that turned this incident into a serious accident was inappropriate operator action, many factors contributed to the action of the operators, such as deficiencies in their training, lack of clarity in their operating procedures, failure of organisations to learn the proper lessons from previous incidents and deficiencies in the design of the control room... Therefore, whether or not operator error explains this particular case, given all the above deficiencies we are convinced that an accident like Three Mile Island was eventually inevitable.

Summary

These accidents reveal that even tried and tested systems can still generate unfortunate errors, and that these often involve an unanticipated sequence of events which culminate in what would have otherwise been an avoidable mistake. Further, accident analysis throws doubt on the traditional fault tree analysis in which the failure rates of components are evaluated independently. This does not appear to be justified in the human case, since minor errors can lead to emotional states which then make other errors more probable. In everyday life it is well known that the performance of even overlearned tasks such as driving can be disrupted by negative criticism, leading to small errors which then disrupt previously successful manoeuvres. Particularly, once an incorrect hypothesis or plan has been formed, then a 'cognitive set' is established which blinds people to the true state of affairs, and prevents them from setting out on a more adaptive course of action.

When the systems which must be controlled are highly complex, then it is possible that operators will be overloaded with information which they will not be able to process, and may rely on inappropriate intuitive judgements (Kahneman and Tversky, 1982). In such situations, operator attempts to cope with the crisis may themselves become a major source of accidents (Perrow, 1984).

A feature of most civilian accidents, even with complex systems, is that some measure of explanation may eventually be found, which may then afford some improvement in safety procedures. In the case of a major nuclear accident no such investigation may ever be possible.

Section 5. **Terrorism**

Few accounts can be found in the open literature on the steps taken by nations to protect their nuclear weapons from falling into the hands of terrorists. The CIA (1976) conducted a study on terrorism, concluding at that time that it would be 'a few years yet' before any terrorist group could manufacture or steal a nuclear weapon. The study added:

> A more likely scenario – at least in the short term – would seem to be a terrorist seizure of a nuclear weapon storage facility or a nuclear power plant in a straightforward barricade operation. Such a group need not threaten a nuclear holocaust (although that possibility would be in the back of everyone's mind), just the destruction of the bunker or reactor with the attendant danger of radiological pollution.

Tactical weapons are admitted to be less securely guarded than strategic weapons. Even these had their security breached on many occasions, and in one publicized lapse, a journalist was able to get a conducted tour of the weak links in the defences by posing as a fencing contractor. He was also sent maps of the nuclear bases, and details of the alarm systems and instructions as to how to obtain security clearance for his supposed construction workers. Shortly after publishing his account of his trips round two nuclear bases, during which he passed near four apparently unguarded hydrogen bombs, steps were reportedly taken to tighten up security, but he still received an unsolicited updated set of blueprints on nuclear bases through the post (*Congressional Record*, 1978).

Not all nuclear weapons have been fitted with anti-terrorist security devices, and therefore many remain in stockpiles, like the Mark 28 hydrogen bomb, which could be opened and reworked by a competent electrician so that it would detonate when dropped from a civilian plane or left in a warehouse. Newer weapons have been fitted with Category D Permissive Action Links, which mean that the bomb cannot easily be detonated without using the proper six-digit code. Military advisers are not keen on what they consider to be too many safeguards, fearing that these will reduce the speed of their nuclear retaliation. Further accounts of breaches of security, and steps being taken to try to counter these can be found in the *Congressional Record* (1978) and Britten (1983).

From the psychological point of view it is a serious omission that lapses of security, highly unreliable behaviour and determined terrorism rarely figure in conventional fault trees, since these constitute a substantial risk. It may be that 'untidy' and malevolent behaviour simply does not fit into the ordered systems of risk assessment which are derived from the world of mechanical components. Whatever the reason, risk analysts often ignore deliberate acts such as terrorism, and planners are said to be very reluctant to consider 'crazy actor dominated' scenarios (Andren, 1981). Yet at the same time there have been 44 terrorist threats involving nuclear weapons in the US in the period 1970–1979. The most credible, which included a workable diagram for a hydrogen bomb, turned out to have been sent by a 14-year-old boy (Britten, 1983). Detailed accounts on the construction of nuclear weapons have been openly published in the US (Britten, 1983), and a postgraduate physicist was able to produce a workable design, starting from scratch, in three months.

Unauthorized possession remains an ever-present and growing risk, since any fissionable material can potentially be turned to explosive purposes, and since there are now over 50,000 nuclear weapons which must be guarded infallibly for ever. Even a 99.9% success rate would leave 50 nuclear weapons at risk.

Section 6. **The command and control of nuclear weapons**

To understand the full range of problems which arise with nuclear weapons it is necessary to move from the study of fallibility in individuals and small groups to the larger problems posed by the interactions of entire nuclear systems.

Bracken (1983) has provided an up to date and comprehensive review of the issues involved in the command and control of nuclear weapons. He argues that understanding the dynamics of how Russian and American nuclear forces perform their functions, how they are organized and which institutional forces shape their mode of operation may be the best way to prevent disaster. By focusing on the management of forces at the moment they go on alert he hopes to identify potential flashpoints and triggers that might lead to catastrophe. Bracken makes the crucial point that there has never been a full scale Russian–American alert.

> No American bombers have been launched in anticipation of an enemy attack, at no time have nuclear weapons in Europe been dispersed from their peacetime storage sites, nor have all of the Soviet nuclear submarines been dispatched from their ports at one time. (*op. cit.*, p.2)

Trying to interpret the present by reference to the past, the likelihood of a nuclear Munich has been exaggerated at the cost of underestimating the probability of a nuclear Sarajevo. In that last instance the institutionalized potential for catastrophe had been built on interlocking alerts and mobilizations that finally swamped the political process. Systems were inflexible, precautionary steps taken by the other side were seen as threatening, and protective reactions spiralled into armed conflict. Bracken points out that in his view a nation's actions in a crisis are more profoundly influenced by the security institutions built up years before the crisis occurs than by the final decisions of obtuse leaders.

> An understanding of how nuclear forces are managed, of how they are alerted, and of how they would be used is necessary if these forces are to be governed in a democratic, or any other kind, of society. (*op. cit.*, p.4)

(i) The American nuclear system

Bracken's characterization of the American warning system is that its complexity soon made it evolve beyond the comprehension of any single person, or even of any small number of people. A torrent of data about Soviet warning systems was obtained by radio and radar intercepts and plane overflights from the early 'fifties, increasing with U2 overflights in June 1956, and mushrooming with the establishment of spy satellites in the 'sixties. The data had to be analyzed and comprehended, and this imposed enormous strains on the intelligence and warning systems. Continuous data monitoring and analysis under a centralized command was the only answer. While nuclear weapons themselves have safety locks on them, it is harder to ensure that similar locks can be placed on the command systems which authorize the use of nuclear weapons.

Since the seventies the presence of Russian submarines capable of firing nuclear missiles at the political command centres in Washington has meant even greater pressure on warning systems, with less time for crucial evaluations and decisions.

The American policy is to deploy weapons widely (though no longer on airborne alert). About 70% of the nuclear submarine fleet is at sea at any one time, compared to about 20% of the Russian fleet. American bombers and land-based missiles appear to be maintained at a higher state of readiness than is the case for the Russian equivalents. America is ahead in computer utilization, and has sought to prevent Russian purchase of such technology in order to maintain its lead.

(ii) The Russian nuclear system

The Russian system, in Bracken's view, shows a reliance on the doctrine of the pre-emptive attack, a consequence of the crippling blows sustained when Germany surprise attacked in 1941. This has led to an increased willingness to contemplate automatic launching procedures, and to the threatened delegation of nuclear firing authority to the generals. Indeed, American sources have claimed that Russia adopted a launch-on-warning policy in the mid 'sixties, by which it is meant that outside peacetime, military operators are given emergency authority to use nuclear weapons if there are indications of an attack. Evaluating the extent to which this differs in practice from NATO contingency plans is not easy. The Russian nuclear system is about 70% land-based, with most of the remaining warheads being sea-based, and only a small proportion deliverable by air. The American system is over 50% sea-based, with the remaining warheads almost equally divided between air and land. Russia is thought to have fewer launchers, and more megatonnage, while America is thought to have more warheads in total, capable of reaching their targets more accurately (SIPRI, 1984). These imbalances profoundly affect negotiating postures, since proposals for any reductions to a class of weapons have different implications for each side. Coupled with the different geographic location of bases, and with the different strategic implications of European missiles for both sides, simple reductions are unlikely to satisfy military planners on either side.

(iii) System interaction

The implications of having two such complex and sensitive interacting warning systems is that small perturbations can be amplified throughout the entire global system, with effects that cannot readily be comprehended even by those closest to the separate command centres. The premium on warning, and the requirement to investigate every defensive precaution as if it were a prelude to attack makes for an inherent instability in the system when fully activated. Yet authoritative spokesmen are generally dismissive when false alerts occur, and make reference to other checks and procedures which, though never fully revealed, should protect the system from inadvertent final activation. Bracken argues that both in the nuclear case and ordinary life, isolated single events rarely cause disasters. A complex system with appropriate checks should survive isolated errors, and in that narrow sense Bracken believes that the likelihood of nuclear war by pure technical accident is lower now than it was 20 years ago. Multiple errors and compound accidents are a different matter. In most human-made disasters there is a series of compound highly correlated events which trigger a sequence of human, bureaucratic and technical reactions. These reactions result in mistaken diagnoses of the problem, leading to steps which may make the matter worse, whilst precious time is lost. The difficulty with human reactions to complex events is that behaviour can develop in unforeseen and unpredictable ways, against which no technical design is proof. Indeed, under those circumstances the sensitivity and complexity of the system may amplify and exacerbate dangerous choices (Perrow, 1984). The present global warning system is the modern equivalent of the interlocking pattern of army mobilizations which created an unstoppable chain reaction of reinforcing alerts and transformed Sarajevo from an isolated assassination to a ruinous major world war. 1914 was not an accident. Everything functioned the way it had been planned to do. Railway timetables began to determine events and only in retrospect can it be seen how war resulted from mobilizations which were intended to be defensive.

At present, nuclear forces are more tightly coupled to the intelligence and warning system than has ever been the case before. The self-correcting option of a loosely coupled system, able to adjust because only a portion of the fighting force has been damaged, is no longer open. Nuclear weapons must be used or lost, and the decision made in less than half an hour.

(iv) Targets and war plans

War plans need to be made to organize the nature of the response to a perceived attack, and, though the details are kept secret, the broad policy outlines eventually get to be discussed by the wider defence community. In essence, as the number of nuclear weapons grew, the concept of specific targetting appeared to become redundant. By 1959, random bombing of Russia would have caused as much damage as any selective bombing policy which used the weapons available. The official position, as stated by Secretary of State Dulles in 1954, was 'massive retaliation', a full scale all-out nuclear attack not necessarily commensurate with the initial Russian provocation. In 1961 Secretary of Defense MacNamara began to search for options which geared the response to the scale of the original attack. The most notable aspect of the new Single Integrated Operational Plan was that Russian cities might be spared as a bargaining counter in negotiations that might take place in a 'small scale' nuclear war. This process was extended further in 1974 by Secretary of Defense Schlesinger to include many more limited nuclear war scenarios, especially for Europe.

By the late 'seventies the Americans had to decide how to target over nine thousand strategic warheads and it was in this context that the ambiguous Presidential Directive PD-59 was signed in July 1980. Some interpreted this as an attempt to plan a war-winning strategy, others saw it as spelling out what had always been assumed, that the political and military control system of the Soviet Union would be targeted, not just Russian military forces. Leitenberg (1981) has argued that American targeting policy has always been directed against such military 'counterforce' targets, and that very little real change has occurred. Since there has always been a gap between the real plans and the publicly declared intentions, it is not suprising that such a fertile confusion should exist. Whatever the public statements, it is conceded that the nuclear arsenal is now big enough for destruction beyond any detailed planning.

Section 7. **The contribution of militarism to fallibility**

The decisions of military staff commanders are prone to the errors which afflict any decision-makers working under stress. Military bureaucracy, however, has its own peculiar social structure. For militarism has become synonymous with complex systems of rewards and punishments designed to foster conformity. These include: the rigid dominance–submission hierarchy; the concern with discipline, over-learned drills and codes of honour; the 'macho' anti-intellectual image; and extreme sensitivity to criticism.

One investigator into the psychology of militarism, Dixon (1976), has analysed the careers of numerous successful and unsuccessful military commanders. Three qualities of decision-making appeared to characterize the most successful (success implies both cool-headed brilliance in strategic planning and humane leadership).

1. The ability to tolerate uncertainty.
2. Spontaneity of thought and action.
3. Keeping minds open to novel and perhaps threatening stimuli.

The problem, as Dixon analyses it, is that these cognitive qualities are totally at odds with the ethics of militarism as described above. There is an even more sinister dimension to military conformity. As Milgram (1974) has pointed out, it encourages an unquestioning compliance with orders. This was the theme of his well-known series of studies, in which two-thirds of normal subjects were willing to administer electric shocks of apparently fatal voltages to another person under the direction of the experimenter. So long as the experimenter was willing to accept responsibility for any injury sustained by the victim, most subjects continued to administer shocks. Such compliance persisted, although at a lower level, when the subject was required to physically hold the subject's arm onto the shock pad.

From these results Milgram concluded:

> This is perhaps the most fundamental lesson in our study: ordinary people, simply doing their jobs, and without any particular hostility on their part, can become agents in a terrible destructive process. (Milgram, 1974)

Milgram wrote against the background of the Vietnam War atrocities such as the My Lai massacre. But his conclusion is just as valid in connection with the possible military use of nuclear weapons.

As the military machine becomes even larger and more complex there will inevitably be greater opportunities for mis-information and mis-communication between different levels within the military hierarchy. The greatest problem is one of upward transmission, particularly when errors need to be reported. Soldiers may be reluctant to admit errors which could lead to disciplinary charges, adverse group pressures, or loss of promotion. The reliability of information flow can also be adversely affected by factors such as personal beliefs, rigid world views, and concepts of loyalty.

Section 8. **Fallibility in political decision-making**

Politicians are ultimately responsible for the deployment of nuclear weapons. To understand their decision-making processes we must first comprehend the social context in which decisions about nuclear armaments are reached. Deutsch (1982) described the system of superpower international relations as what he terms a 'malignant social process'.

> The superpowers are involved in a crazy social process, which, given the existence of nuclear weapons, is too dangerous to allow to continue. Perfectly sane and intelligent people, once they are enmeshed in a crazy social process, may engage in actions which seem to them completely rational and necessary, but which a detached, objective, observer would readily identify as contributing to the perpetuation and intensification of a vicious cycle of interactions. (Deutsch, 1983)

He defines such a process as one

> which is increasingly dangerous and costly to the participants and from which the participants see no way of extricating themselves without leaving themselves vulnerable to an unacceptable loss in a value central to their self-identities or self-esteem. (Deutsch, 1983)

Some characteristics of such processes are:

1. Being involved in an anarchic social situation.
2. A competitive orientation to one another.
3. Cognitive rigidity within the parties.
4. Misperceptions.
5. Unwitting commitments.
6. Self-fulfilling prophecies.
7. Vicious escalating spirals. (Deutsch, 1983)

Anarchic social situations have been explored in experimental laboratory games of trust and suspicion (Deutsch, 1958). The essential psychological point is this: when there is no trust that the other side will 'play by the rules', there is no possibility that either party will behave rationally. Distrust leads to competition and attempts by each side to achieve maximum gain at the expense of its opponent. Yet only cooperation can secure the most favourable outcomes (Dawes, 1980). A key example here is the havoc that mutual suspicion has wrought on the Soviet–American disarmament talks over the years.

Competitiveness between the superpowers is usually explained in terms of incompatible ideologies: capitalism versus communism. However, a number of workers have pointed out intriguing 'mirror-image' aspects of the views of leading Soviet and American analysts. As Milburn *et al.* (1982) point out:

> All believe that the leadership of their major adversary is monolithic and that there are essentially no differences among members of the ruling class of their opponents... Those on the ideological right in both countries argue for the obstinate, stubborn immutability of their imperialistic opposite number...

Over 20 years ago, Bronfenbrenner (1961) described the similar 'mirror-image' views found among ordinary Russians and their American counterparts. He utilizes three social phenomena to explain such rigid and distorted perceptions.

1. The cognitive dissonance literature (Festinger, 1957) provides ample evidence of the powerful 'strain to consistency' in social relations. This happens through our tendency to reduce life's inconsistencies and complexities to the simplest frames of reference; for example, 'goodies and baddies'. Such cognitive rigidity is especially strong under conditions of stress.

2. These mechanisms are reinforced by the pressure to social conformity typified by the 'Asch phenomenon' (Asch, 1956), in which subjects altered their stated judgements in a simple perceptual task when stooges working for the experimenter called out obviously wrong answers.

3. To add to the possible distortions, one side's misperceptions of the other can result in a self-fulfilling prophecy. That is, the other side is likely to respond in a way that appears to justify the original misperception. Such self-fulfilling prophecies help to perpetuate a freeze in superpower relations.

This can be illustrated with the following example: in an atmosphere of international suspicion, Superpower A announces an increase in its nuclear arsenal. Superpower B reciprocates by announcing that it will add to its arsenal to prevent A 'getting ahead'. This move then reinforces A's suspicion of B's imperialistic intentions.

This situation is similar to the familiar one encountered in clinical practice in which the wife asserts 'I shout at him because he never talks to me' and the husband replies 'I don't feel like talking after she's shouted at me'. The essence of this misunderstanding is that both parties identify different starting points. They both feel entirely in the right because the apparent sequence of events seems to justify their interpretations, but any outsider can see that they are locked into a vicious cycle. Over the last 10 years, a new area of psychological research has grown up around the notion of psychological entrapment: our capacity to persist in plans which are clearly failing (e.g. Rubin, 1981).

Experimental work has investigated the factors which determine whether people decide to persist in a failing course of action, or cut their losses. One model (Levi, 1981) suggests that, paradoxically, the strength of the tendency to persist is directly proportional to the perceived magnitude of losses already incurred. This may throw some light on the conduct of both Argentina and Great Britain at different stages of the South Atlantic conflict.

In times of conflict, politicians tend to make decisions in small war cabinets. Groups can be fallible in distinctive ways. The peculiarities of group political decision-making have been explored by Janis (1972), who has made case-studies of various historical crises and identified six symptoms of 'Group-Think' which contribute to faulty decision-making processes:

1. An illusion of invulnerability that becomes shared by most members of the group.
2. Collective attempts to ignore or rationalize away items of information challenging shaky but cherished assumptions.
3. An unquestioned belief in the group's inherent morality.
4. Stereotyping the enemy as either too evil for negotations or too stupid to be a threat.
5. A shared illusion of unanimity in a majority viewpoint.
6. Self-appointed 'mind-guards' to protect the group from adverse information.

These findings indicate that fallible decision-making is likely under conditions of stress, and that time pressure exacerbates the problem of irrational and dangerous decisions.

Section 9. **The risks of accidental nuclear war**

Britten (1983) in a major review of the risks of nuclear war, feels that although US nuclear weapons safety has undoubtedly improved greatly, there is an over-reliance on supposedly 'hard data' from fault tree analyses, a mistaken belief in human rationality, and the ever-present hazard of complacency.

> Despite the improvement in safety measures, it is disquieting to find that the note of confident reassurance that pervades much of the writing and most government pronouncements on nuclear weapons safety today is no different from that of the mid 1960's. By then some serious faults in physical security and administrative procedures had been brought to light and corrected, but there were some extremely serious accidents yet to come. (p.43)

Britten also makes the point that nuclear weapons impose a risk on citizens which they are in no position to evaluate, since the facts are not made known to them.

Frei (1983) has reviewed the issue of accidental nuclear war for the United Nations, and as an official publication his review merits particular attention. He used the phrase 'unintentional nuclear war' to cover the following three types of war:

(i) a nuclear war initiated independently of any explicit decision by the legitimate authorities;

(ii) a nuclear war initiated deliberately and voluntarily by legitmate authorities but based on false assumptions;

(iii) a war of greater intensity and scope than was envisaged by those who made the decision to use force, e.g. a war escalating from conventional warfare into a nuclear exchange not foreseen by the opposing sides.

He then takes an overview of the principles of the contending parties using paradigms such as the Prisoner's Dilemma Game and other strategy and game theory approaches to the nuclear arms race and to a nuclear confrontation. One feature which dominates the discussion is the growing urgency generated by the shrinking of the time available between warning and the impact of offensive missiles. This time has been rapidly dwindling in recent years as a result of technological innovations. It is said to be less than 30 minutes for land-based strategic missiles, 15 minutes for submarine launched missiles and less than 8 minutes for shorter range missiles such as the SS20 and Pershing II. According to the United States Office of Technology Assessment (1981) the time available for deciding on a response to a Soviet attack could range from an upper limit of 20 minutes to no time at all. They further stress that meeting this deadline is dependent upon provisional planning by the President and his advisers. Frei goes on to discuss the dangers of the launch-on-warning policy and examines some of the other options such as the Pre-Delegation of launch capability to units operating in the field.

In attempting to discuss the pressures which might lead to unintentional war he quotes the view of Barnaby (1981) that military technology has its own momentum which is largely outside direct political control, and that there is an increasing inducement, with larger and more accurate destructive weapons, to go for a first strike policy – the 'use them or lose them' policy.

Frei makes reference to psychological variables discussed above, such as 'Group-Think', and the inflexibiliy of standard operating procedures. Discussing 'Group-Think' he points out that there is a tendency among top decision makers to surround themselves with advisers whose main function is a psychologically supportive role. This tendency minimizes objective and critical evaluation of decisions. Under the heading of Standard Operating procedures he quotes the work of Betts (1977) on the Cuban missile crisis, showing that the American Navy's conduct of the blockade was determined more by navy regulations than by the needs of the US government. These differences resulted in severe internal arguments during the crisis as to the precise location of the blockade ships and the reaction which would be taken if a Soviet ship refused to divulge its cargo. The inertia of overlearned bureaucratic procedures can be a major contributor to inappropriate and dangerous responses.

On the human factor, Frei notes the reports about alcoholism, drug addiction and mental illness but seems to feel that these are adequately covered by technological devices which control the activation of warheads. His view is that the existing safeguards practically exclude any serious accident or incident due to technological failure or malfunction. Details of the safeguards are not given.

After a quite extensive review of literature, Frei reaches his final conclusion, which is that the overall risk of unintentional nuclear war is minimal if expressed as a percentage probability. He rates this probability as 'almost close to zero'.

There then follows a one-page appendix entitled 'The Tentative, Quantitative Evaluation of the Risk of Unintentional Nuclear War' which was written by Dr Sontag, presumably based on work done in 1981 (Frei, p.222). This one-page appendix makes no direct reference to the foregoing text and states that 'the following calculations are based on very crude and subjective estimates that cannot be confirmed or refuted by any empiricial evidence'. This constitutes an extraordinary statement, and means that the figures cannot be subjected to any meaningful analysis. However, even the table itself seems to have been misunderstood by Frei. Without any explanation, or any linkage to the factors mentioned in the book, Sontag attempts to estimate the probability of a major nuclear war within five years. Under normal conditions the probability is given as one in a hundred, and under crisis conditions as one in twenty. These probabilities are naturally extremely high in actuarial terms, bearing in mind the nature of the risk, and it seems that Frei has misunderstood the notation used for probability estimates. This is the only possible explanation for drawing such reassuring conclusions from such alarming estimates.

In evaluating Frei's text, it can be said that it enumerates risks without any detailed attempts at estimating their magnitude. The figures in the appendix do not appear to relate in any clear way to the many risk-producing factors discussed in the text. These figures from the appendix seem to have been misinterpreted, and to have been incorporated in misunderstood form in Frei's conclusions.

A recent working party on problems of rational decision-making (IPPNW, 1983), which included Western and Russian scientists and physicians, took the view that the risk of accidental nuclear war was substantial. Kabanov (1983) was unable to provide data on Russian military drug abuse or selection procedures, but admitted an alcoholism problem in the civilian population. Weizenbaum (1983) drew attention to the fact that when major computer systems become established within large organizations they become very difficult to change, since even minor programming alterations may have major unintended effects. Organizations are reluctant to risk losing a computer service on which they have become dependent, and generally prefer to circumvent shortcomings in the system, thus perpetuating errors.

Bracken (1983) has drawn attention to the great dangers which arise when nuclear systems go on alert and Bereanu (1983) suggests that the present global nuclear system is now close to being a self-activating stockpile.

Cull *et al.* (1983) have summarized the major areas in which errors can occur which could lead to unintended nuclear explosion, but do not attempt to calculate probabilities. They list the following areas in which faults and difficulties might lead to an unplanned nuclear explosion:

1. signal detection by warning systems;
2. communication with decision makers;
3. response selection by decision makers;
4. communication with executors;
5. execution of command (a) warhead assembly, (b) vehicle readiness, (c) target selection;
6. maintaining all systems;
7. guarding all systems.

On the basis of what is known about human fallibility, they outlined a likely scenario for a major nuclear accident.

1. Superpowers in a state of tension.
2. An ambiguous military event or error causes a high state of alert.
3. Readiness is maintained whilst negotations continue inconclusively.
4. Partial reduction of the state of alert is agreed. Decision-makers are tense, and under pressure not to give way, command crews are highly aroused and emotionally exhausted.
5. A second error occurs.

It can be seen that this illustrative example assumes that a state of tension exists in which accidental events are interpreted as having malevolent intentions. The subsequent state of alert makes people feel that they are under real threat, and consequently they are more likely to do what they are told is necessary in order to defend themselves. Inconclusive negotiations maintain anxiety and reduce trust. A partial relaxation leads to error-prone behaviour at a time when nuclear weapons are primed and loaded. This second error is misinterpreted.

This example follows the analysis of accidents in assuming that it is a chain of events, each of which is considered improbable, which eventually leads to a high probability of an accident despite all precautions.

A long established consensus measure of the overall risk of nuclear war has been provided by the *Bulletin of the Atomic Scientists*, who in 1947 set their 'doomsday clock' at seven minutes before midnight. The clock moved as close as two minutes to midnight in 1953 when the USSR detonated their first hydrogen bomb, and as far away as twelve minutes in 1972 when the SALT 1 treaty was signed. The present estimate, on the advice of 47 scientists (including 18 Nobel prize-winners) sets the clock forward to three minutes before midnight, the closest it has been for 30 years (*Bulletin of the Atomic Scientists*, 1983).

Conclusions

Human fallibility is such that no enterprise can ever be error-free. Many factors make for errors in skilled performance, and when these are coupled with the difficulties of making rational decisions under stress and time pressure, the risks of accidental nuclear war are seen to be more substantial than officially admitted. Drug abuse may contribute considerably to dangerous accidents. Only one nuclear nation has provided figures on the extent of this problem in its service personnel, and the findings are a cause for considerable concern. Until other nuclear nations provide their figures, the full extent of the problem will not be known. Mechanical safeguards cannot totally overcome un-reliable behaviour, especially during nuclear alerts. It is not possible to make a detailed analysis of the risk without understanding fully the operating systems of the nuclear powers, and such data are not available. Conversely, it is possible to evaluate the governmental statements about the improbability of nuclear war in the light of what is known about all other human ventures where safety is at a premium. Any study of accidents reveals that although certain accidents can be minimized by appropriate procedures, the possibility of accident can never be excluded even from the most carefully constructed system. No data have been presented which would show that nuclear nations have solved this problem. Since every citizen is placed under risk by these weapons, it is encumbent upon them to provide full data on their safety procedures.

When there are over 50,000 nuclear weapons to be guarded the danger of terrorism cannot be discounted. With the spread of knowledge about nuclear matters, all fissile material must be considered a terrorist risk.

When the full range of human behaviours and motivations is considered, the possibility of unintentional nuclear war can be seen to be greater than that proposed by official fault trees with their largely error-free and benignly disposed human operators.

5

NEGOTIATIONS AND CONFLICT RESOLUTION

It is not possible within the compass of this statement to cover adequately a field which includes so much psychological and historical material. A few main points will be made to highlight the psychological features of international bargaining, and to show possible avenues for productive negotiations on the issue of nuclear disarmament. The field of negotiations has been well studied by Morley and Stephenson (1977), and Tysoe (1982) has provided a recent review of bargaining. Actual crises have been studied by Hermann (1972), Brecher (1978), and Janis (1972), and Wilkenfeld and Brecher (1982). A general outline of psychology's contribution to crisis and conflict resolution has been given by Oppenheim (1984), whose general explanatory framework will be followed in the introductory section.

Psychology's contribution to international conflict resolution

Psychologists accustomed to the study of individuals may well feel that the field of international relations is too broad and complex for meaningful psychological analysis. Pure experimentation is certainly not possible, and the avenues appear to be either an empirical approach to actual conflicts, interviewing participants, analysing documents and communiqués; or simulating life-like negotiations under some experimental constraints. Psychologists have generally been unwilling to go beyond the study of small groups, since the issues raised by international relations appear vague, out-of-bounds and unresearchable.

In the early 'sixties scholars in international research became more interested in behavioural approaches while a few social psychologists, aware of the dangers of nuclear war, lent their skills and theories to the new field.

Game theory, as a form of conflict simulation, began to be more widely used, and current work includes analysis of each participant's perception of the game, rather than assuming that all are playing by the same rules (Bennett and Dando, 1983). Such simulations showed how both parties could get into a competitive framework which drew them into greater threat.

New forms of analysis, which gave more place to psychological variables, were applied to the study of crises, and problem-solving workshops were initiated as a means of resolving conflicts (Burton, 1979). Despite this, much of this academic work has been limited in scope and has not addressed itself to issues such as perceptions of national interest, bureaucratic politics within governments, or the influence of the defence industry.

However, it remains the case that decisions are taken not by disembodied powers but by people, generally working in small groups. Because of this, it is possible to conduct psychological studies without necessarily having to investigate the attitudes and functioning of entire nations. In the words of a leading researcher 'there is an irreducibly psychological component' involved in negotiations (Morley, 1979, p.214).

Even the most prominent decision-makers are more fallible than their publicity machines would have us believe, and they are subject to prejudice, false hypotheses, lapses of attention and memory, lack of practice and plain ignorance. Also, the decision-maker must operate within an organization, the nature and structure of which will mould the decisions which can be taken.

Much psychological work can be done beyond attempts to analyse the personalities of national leaders. The plan of this section is first to study crises, which are the most obvious breakpoints in peaceful relations between nations, and as such attract both public and research interest. Crises will be described in terms of how they influence and are seen by the participants, and some general points will be made about crisis prevention. Then further points will be made about negotiations, and some proposals for improved negotiations discussed.

Section 1. **Psychological aspects of crisis behaviour**

The reactions which people show to stress follow a curvilinear path. As arousal increases, performance improves. People are motivated to perform well. As arousal increases even further, they pass through a plateau, and then their performance begins to deteriorate. At the highest levels of stress skilled performance breaks down. Similarly, the initial stages of a crisis can be stimulating, but if it continues or becomes more

severe then disintegration of performance is likely (Oppenheim, 1984). Brecher (1978) suggests that four main factors create a crisis:
1.   high threat – ultimately about survival;
2.   great uncertainty – about opponent's intentions and capabilities;
3.   severe time pressure – in which there is urgency about decisions;
4.   fear of disunity – in which common aims must be maintained under pressure.

Although a major crisis will be felt by all citizens, as the crisis proceeds and decisions are referred upwards, fewer and fewer people will be able to affect its course, until in extreme cases the main effects are felt by a small isolated group of decision-makers.

Cognitive and perceptual processes during crises

Crises can be conceived of as a transition zone between peace and war (Snyder, 1972) which brings out behaviours typical of both conditions in an uneasy mixture. The following remarks outline the main features of most crises.

Crises have to be created, and that requires antagonistic parties to make a show of their antagonism. People posture, threaten, close ranks and goad the opposition into response. At this stage the procedure may seem unreal and intrinsically safe, since the antagonistic behaviour may not yet be fully meant.

Perceptions become polarized. Things are seen in black and white terms, bad qualities are projected onto the other side and failings on one's own side, even if highly relevant to the crisis, are overlooked. Oskamp (1965) found that American students were more favourably disposed to US actions such as increasing military spending and making disarmament proposals, than towards identical actions from the USSR. Each may see the other as bent on world domination, and as being so uncivilized as not to be capable of serious negotiation. This mirror-image effect (Bronfenbrenner, 1961) affects all perceptions of the other party's actions. These hostile images may serve as a preparation for the use of force, which is 'justified' by these projections of evil (Fisher, 1969).

These perceptions on the part of politicians have been studied by means of cognitive maps. Previous studies of the psychological makeup of prominent politicians have generally left a gap between personal characteristics and actual behaviour under political stress. This gap can begin to be bridged by the study of the attitudes, beliefs and preferred modes of operation of the decision-makers. Such studies provide cognitive maps (Axelrod, 1976) of the politicians' mental world, of what they believe to be 'the lessons of history', of their basic values and how they see their allies and opponents. These maps assist in understanding likely reactions to the moves being made by other politicians on the international scene. They cannot totally determine how a politician will react in a crisis, but they give a more detailed view than could be gained from a study of individual personality.

Conflict rhetoric is set in motion. This appeals to emotion, not reason, and depends upon previously established national identities based on flags, anthems, and ceremonies so as to condition strong emotional responses which wipe out rational consideration of the case in question. For this rhetoric to be effective it is necessary for previous work to have been done to establish a national identity. Little distinction is drawn between the actions of foreign military groups and the supposed personality characteristics of entire nations. Gallup (1972) has repeatedly polled US public opinion on the characteristics of people from other nations. In 1942 Germans and Japanese were seen as warlike, treacherous and cruel, while none of these descriptions were applied to the Russians, who were allies at that time. By 1966 those descriptions were not used of the Germans and the Japanese, but the Russians were seen as warlike and treacherous. The Chinese were similarly described, with the additional racial stereotype of being 'sly'. After President Nixon's trip to China they were then described as hard-working, intelligent, artistic, progressive and practical. As Frank (1982) points out, the primitive image of 'the enemy', which arises out of fear and distrust, is always virtually the same, and is applied to rival groups regardless of reality. National-centrism is deliberately escalated in circumstances of threat so as to motivate and coordinate potential warlike actions.

Strong social forces are needed to unify a group of individuals so that they take on a special identity. This can be done by consciousness raising, speeches, popular books, films, songs and all the paraphernalia of nationalism. Dean Rusk (1984), a former US Secretary of State, speaking of the unusual levels of acrimony of current US–USSR rhetoric warned: 'there is a self-hypnotic effect in rhetoric that could cause one or both to begin to believe their own excessive vituperation and lead to dangers that we ought to try to avoid'.

Options for reducing the crisis are narrowed down to 'one way out'. Long range multi-option planning is abandoned, and practical short-term matters predominate in people's thoughts.

Communication with the other side breaks down, and their viewpoint can no longer be seen. The other side is seen as treacherous and malevolent. 'At the very moment when they most need to engage in subtle consideration and awareness of each other's thought processes they will break off all communications and withdraw their ambassadors' (Oppenheim, 1984).

The need for unity becomes so pressing that bad decisions may be made simply to maintain a common front, and internal divisions must be papered over. Images which unite the country and stifle doubts are propagated by the mass media. These stress the inherent morality of the nation, and question the morality of the opposition. Such propaganda buttresses decision-makers at a time of stress and doubt, and steps may be taken to suppress information and any discussion which questions the decisions taken. Dissenters may be seen as traitors.

Crises generate more information, at more speed, and of more importance than that of normal day to day events, and this causes an information explosion. More personnel will be needed, telex and telephone will replace letter writing, and new organizational procedures may be needed in order to process and respond to all the messages being received. As a consequence of this, and the time pressure, decision-makers will find themselves in a condition of overload. Holsti (1972) studied the crises of 1914 and 1962 (Cuban missiles) in terms of time constraints, alternatives and communications. In a very detailed analysis of historical records, communiqués and personal accounts, he showed that time pressures certainly contributed to the breakdown of the 1914 negotiations, but that the conscious attempt to cope with these may have brought about the peaceful resolution of the 1962 crisis. Certainly President Kennedy had the errors of 1914 in mind during the crisis, as well as the more recent personal fiasco of the Bay of Pigs invasion attempt less than two years before. Despite all attempts to provide adequate thinking time for both parties, the pressure was intense. Robert Kennedy, who was involved throughout the crisis, recalled 'some [American decision-makers] because of the pressure of events, even appeared to lose their judgment and stability' (Kennedy, 1969, p.6). Krushchev's message of 26th October, never published, is said by some of those that have seen it to reveal the incoherence of a person on the verge of total collapse (Holsti, 1972).

During a crisis there will be too many facts to be taken in and considered, and too little time in which to do this, and formulate considered replies. Instead of up to date facts being discussed calmly by several groups of advisers, each able to express an independent view, the decision-makers during a crisis may have to make sense of news which has already been overtaken by events, and do so hurriedly on their own, or with a few key advisers, in a situation where a particular policy must be upheld at all costs. Coupled to this they will have little time for sleeping, eating and reflecting on matters away from the atmosphere of the crisis control rooms. If, in addition, they have had to travel by plane across time zones, then the disruption of circadian rhythms may further reduce their capacity to function as rational and calm people (Colquhoun, 1971). They will have to weather the impact of the main components of any crisis: high stakes, extreme urgency, great uncertainty, and the threat of internal disunity (Brecher, 1978).

Experiences of crisis participants

The experience of being in such a crisis has been recounted by participants, who have been interviewed afterwards, and who have been able to go through the communiqués with the investigators. Brecher (1978) made a very detailed study of Arab–Israeli conflicts in which almost an hour by hour account was available from the major participants. Simulation work has also provided validatory data, so that the main features of all crises have been established. Oppenheim (1984) has given an account of the main findings.

Decision-makers start to experience stress as the crisis develops. In the very early stages this may be pleasurable, since it gives politicians a sense of importance and expands their roles. They may be able to act brusquely and cut through red tape, and may enjoy the sense of teamwork which builds up as everyone gets to work. As the crisis deepens their thinking becomes polarized and oversimplified, with emotional overtones. They develop tunnel vision, becoming unable to see the other side's point of view. They give short-term objectives precedence over long-term goals, even though the short-term objective may run counter to what they wish to achieve in the long run. They find it difficult to generate a range of solutions to the problem, but tend to persist with the few they originally proposed, and find that they cannot anticipate counter-moves. Their powers of concentration begin to fail as stress builds up. Anxiety increases, mostly caused by uncertainty, and thinking becomes more rigid. Unity is seen as absolutely essential, and a feeling of urgency pervades, in which delays in decision making are seen as fatal. They show the reactions common in conditions of sustained threat, when even bad news is better than no news at all, because it signals an eventual end to intolerable stress. Information from the other side is distrusted, and seen in a fear-distorted way, and as a consequence participants tend to respond with exorbitant bargaining positions, rather than realistic compromises, which thus make the crisis worse.

Interestingly, it is a common experience of participants in a disastrous crisis that after it is all over they cannot understand how it all came about (Janis, 1972). This underlines the importance of group processes in giving meaning, and a shared sense of importance, to the events which constituted the crisis. The crisis takes on a life of its own because the participants are willing to believe in it, and take its urgency seriously. In a sense, most crises in history could be described not as *'folies à deux'*, but essentially as the madness of roughly the two dozen people involved in the key war cabinets.

Organizations respond to crises by working harder in the apparently essential areas and ignoring other duties, by adapting internal procedures so as to speed up decision-making, and by trying to service the needs of the key 'war cabinet' who unfortunately may be too busy or too defensive to maintain their usual receptivity to advice. Few countries can afford to have permanent high level crisis management teams, let alone the two alternating teams used by the US to maximize their negotiating performance during the Cuban missile crisis (Oppenheim, 1984).

Section 2. **Historical background**

Arms races in history

Lazlo and Keys (1981) have studied major wars (defined as over 1000 battle deaths) in the period 1816 to 1965, measuring the duration of and number of countries involved in each war, and the total casualties. They found that if a randomly selected pair of major powers found themselves in a military confrontation then they had an 11% probability of going to war, yet if they also happened to be engaged in an arms race, then the likelihood of war was 80%.

Eberwein (1981), using the same database, reports that military confrontations escalate within 14 days to war, or not at all. This suggests that pressure of time has an important effect on decision-making in crisis, and that the relatively immediate, time-pressured, often emotional response, may be the determining one (Holsti, 1972).

In the case of the North Korean invasion of South Korea, the US decision to go to war was taken in six days. The war lasted three years, and was the fifth most costly, in terms of casualties, in American history (Paige, 1972).

Wallace (1981), using the same data, investigated the theory that if you want peace you should prepare for war. He used an arms race index based on the product of the rate of arms growth for pairs of contending states over a 10-year period prior to the involvement in a serious dispute or military confrontation. He found that this arms race index predicted

23 out of 26 war escalations and 63 out of 73 peaceful outcomes. Further analyses of the data suggest that the *'para bellum'* hypothesis is disproved.

The suggestion which comes from this work is that the preparatory activities of investing resources in weaponry, and the training of people to use these weapons, facilitates the decision to use them in a crisis.

Historical background to Russian–American relations

Since relations between the superpowers are a key issue in nuclear negotiations, the sense of history which both parties bring to the conference table is psychologically important.

Prins *et al.* (1982) have given an account of Russo–American relations which they characterize as a trail of mistrust. The crisis of disillusion and exhaustion towards the end of the First World War led to revolution in Russia, and the threat of it in other countries. Under Lenin Russia sued for peace, and the Western powers were as much angered by their withdrawal as with any challenge posed by Marxism. When Russia was embroiled in a bloody civil war the West intervened on the side of the Whites, and American, British, French and Japanese troops landed in Russia in an attempt to crush the Reds. The intervention failed, and whilst to the West this was a minor episode, in Russia it kindled a deep suspicion of the West (with whom there had been relatively little contact), and a fear of encirclement which has never died.

By the early 'thirties Russia had established trade and diplomatic relations with Europe, and was embarked on a painful process of rapid enforced industrialization. America refused to extend diplomatic recognition for 15 years, even after Stalin had defeated Trotsky and his concept of international revolution, and was following the policy of 'socialism in one country'. The American view was that communism was an unworkable system, and recognition would only postpone its inevitable collapse. America had a policy of isolationism, and with the rise of Nazism in Germany, Russia sought to create an anti-fascist grouping with other European nations. These were unwilling to join forces with a country they distrusted, and part of the policy of appeasement was the hope that fascism and communism would turn on each other. When eventually Stalin sided with Hitler, feelings of suspicion and distrust were confirmed.

The Second World War was one which both Russia and America did not wish to join, but into which they were eventually thrown by suffering surprise attacks. Russia paid an enormous price for being caught by surprise, and within a few weeks almost lost everything which had been achieved since the revolution. Millions were taken prisoner, cities destroyed or besieged, until the reorganized Russian army finally evicted the invaders, having taken on the major part of the German army. The seven and a half million soldiers who died represented 1 in 22 of the population, and there were an additional 12 million civilian deaths. The trauma bound government and people together in nationalistic patriotism, and made a deep and lasting impression on the Russian nation.

America suffered no mainland casualties or destruction, and lost 405,000 soldiers. The economy boomed while Europe destroyed itself, and it emerged from the war as the undisputed world power.

The peoples of both nations have a totally dissimilar experience of war, and this contributes to the distinct psychological perspectives which each side brings to international relations.

It is extremely difficult to give an account of the subsequent history of Soviet–American relations which does not take on the descriptive framework of either side.

History of US–USSR confrontation

Since the historical accounts of superpower confrontation are themselves highly politicized, it is useful to attempt to use common standards, and an openly available database, to discern long-term trends. Wilkenfeld and Brecher (1982) have used the International Crisis Behaviour project database CRISBANK to study the 39 US and 20 USSR crises in the period 1945 to 1975. International crises are defined as times when the nation's highest decision-makers perceive a high probability of military hostilities, a threat to basic values and a finite time for response. The authors have sought to identify the trigger to the crisis, the issue it involved, the value of the threat involved, the technique of crisis management and the extent of violence.

Wilkenfeld and Brecher found that triggers resulting from indirect violent military action, not directly involving either superpower, constituted the largest category of crises. The USSR did not perceive a crisis for itself in any of the indirect violence cases in which the US had become involved. The US on the other hand saw a crisis for itself in five of the seven cases of USSR involvement.

Whereas other countries have acted to protect territory, influence, political systems, economic interests and their very existence, the threat to the superpowers was almost exclusively to their influence. The data reveal diversity for each superpower as well as considerable differences between them. For the USSR 50% of its crises reflect a concern for potential decline within its own bloc, whereas this accounts for only 5% of US cases. For the USSR these cases included the early communist takeovers in Eastern Europe, and subsequent interventions, while for the US, crises in Korea were the sole cases of within-bloc concern. This suggests, Wilkenfeld and Brecher argue, that the USSR is much less secure in its control over its bloc than the US. The US is more concerned about potential loss of influence among non-bloc client and nonaligned states, which accounts for 56% of cases, whereas the USSR reflects this concern in only 25% of its cases.

The crisis management techniques used by the superpowers are shown in the table below.

Table 5. Primary crisis management techniques used in crises

Techniques	US cases	USSR cases
Negotiation	11	2
Multiple non-violent	10	4
Military non-violent	5	9
Nonmilitary pressure	1	0
Violence	9	2
Multiple including violence	3	3

(adapted from Wilkenfeld and Brecher, Table 8.5)

Wilkenfeld and Brecher note that in proportional terms the US has used more negotiation and violence, while the USSR has more often used military non-violent techniques, particularly following the end of the Second World War when consolidating communist regimes in Eastern Europe.

When these crises are categorized according to the extent of violence, it is found that the superpowers resorted rather sparingly to extensive violence as a crisis management technique.

Table 6. Extent of violence as crisis management technique

Extent of violence	US cases	USSR cases
Exclusive	5	2
Central, + other techniques	7	2
Minor role	1	1
No role	26	15

(adapted from Wilkenfeld and Brecher, p.195)

Turning to crisis outcome, the authors find that in all five US–USSR confrontations the USSR was defeated (Iran 1946, Berlin blockade 1948, Cuba 1962, Stanleyville, Congo 1964, Six-Day War 1967), while in none of the five US defeats was the USSR a crisis actor. Clearly, the US has had the upper hand in crisis confrontations between the superpowers.

The 30-year period under study has seen a change in the status of the USSR. In the period 1945 to 1962 crises were bipolar, from 1963 to 1975 they were polycentric.

Turning to the crucial issue of the relationship between crisis technique and outcome, Wilkenfeld and Brecher reach several conclusions in their study. First, the international system is dominated by the US and its interests. The US never experienced defeat at the hands of the USSR, while all cases of USSR defeat involved direct crisis confrontation with the US. US employment of extreme forms of violence as crisis management techniques, particularly when confronting the USSR, tended to enhance goal achievement. A significant shift began to occur in US fortunes after 1963, in which US crises were of longer duration and were less successful, even when extreme violence was employed.

The USSR exhibited a singular inability to manage military–security crises to its advantage. The overwhelmingly important feature of USSR crisis behaviour is the threat of decline in its influence within its own bloc.

For both superpowers, violence paid in crisis situations. Finally, the authors point out that, although there are always features which make individual crises unique, important strands of regularity can be found in the behaviour of states in the international system.

These regularities constitute the organizational norms within which individual decision-makers must operate. They provide the national 'cognitive map' within which the psychological viewpoint of particular key people are contained. US decision-makers appear to have a wider world view, and are more successful, while USSR decision-makers have a more defensive orientation, and have often been defeated when confronting the US.

Section 3. **Crisis prevention**

The likelihood of violent conflicts can be reduced by developing the skills of crisis avoidance. At an institutional level, the bureaucratic systems responsible for dealing with crises can be given better communication capacity, higher staffing levels and the freedom from operating constraints needed to develop less rigid responses.

Personnel can be selected who are most likely to be calm under stress and have flexible coping styles with the capacity to think several moves ahead. These executives can be trained by simulation exercises in order to practice their skills. One technique is the use of problem solving workshops (Burton, 1979), which seek to re-establish severed communications, counteract narrowed and polarized perceptions, deflate conflict rhetoric while helping the parties discover underlying and hitherto inadmissible motives, and try to establish an atmosphere of trust. In the language of games theory, they try to turn the conflict from zero sum to positive sum, in which all participants gain. These workshops avoid legalistic and territorial concerns and concentrate on needs, fears and perceptions. Participants find the process liberating, and often have problems when they return to their original groupings where the old antagonistic attitudes prevail. These have not yet been fully evaluated in terms of the subsequent performance of the participants.

Current crisis prevention relies on old solutions such as alliances, balances of power and idealized solutions such as international law. More productive solutions might lie in treaties of common security, supported by practical arrangements which provide more flexibility.

Negotiation

Negotiation has been defined as verbal communication which parties undertake in order jointly to resolve a conflict of interest between them. Negotiation involves the parties in mixed motives – the motive to gain a settlement maximally favourable to themselves, and the motive to cooperate in order to reach a settlement at all (Morley and Stephenson, 1977).

Experimental paradigms used to study negotiating have ranged from simple zero sum games (what one party wins the other loses) through positive sum games (in which, through cooperation, it is possible for both to gain something) to role-playing debates. The results of these simulated negotiations have been analysed in many ways, but the detailed content analysis technique, Conference Process Analysis, is probably the most satisfactory, though very elaborate. It is described fully by Morley and Stephenson (1977).

Negotiations tend to follow a common sequence. Before the negotiations proceed, the negotiators meet with their own party in caucus to discuss their position, which tends to enhance negotiator commitment, and make agreement less likely (Fischoff, 1972; Louche, 1975). This effect may be even stronger where national constituencies are involved.

Then negotiations about negotiations take place. These attempt to decide who will be represented, in what capacity, and with what status. The Paris negotiations on Vietnam were held up by a dispute on the status of the Viet Cong representatives, since to recognize them as national representatives would have been to concede one of the issues over which the war was being fought.

Then negotiations must take place as to the agenda. Decisions must be made as to whether related issues are to be considered together, or in separate conferences. There is evidence that taking several issues together leads to faster decisions than arguing each issue separately, since package deals of concessions can be agreed more easily (Tysoe, 1982).

Other features of negotiations can be obtained from the more accessible and widely studied field of industrial negotiations. Douglas (1957, 1962) found that negotiators reached agreement by passing through three distinct phases. The first, which she called 'establishing the bargaining range', consisted of full statements of positions from both parties, with attacks upon the statements of the other side. not personal, but directed against the position of a party. Morley and Stephenson (1977) add that, at this stage, the parties test the relative strengths of the cases and their relative capacity to inflict damage on the other side if there is deadlock.

The second phase was 'reconnoitering the range', in which options were explored and attempts made to get a favourable position within the range. The third and final phase was 'precipitating the decision-making crisis' as options were closed off and a settlement was forced.

Finally, once a settlement has been reached, negotiators must return to their wider constituencies, and convince them that they have acted in their best interests. The constituents may still be caught in the emotional effects of the rhetoric of conflict, and may have difficulty adjusting to the more limited and rational goals which have been obtained.

Initiatives in disarmament negotiations

The history of negotiations on nuclear disarmament has been very disappointing. Leitenberg (1978) has argued that US–USSR negotiations have generally served only to legitimize and institutionalize military preparations which have continued unabated since the Second World War. Not one single nuclear weapon, missile, aircraft, ship, tank or rifle has been destroyed by agreement between the two countries. Public disarmament proposals have generally been for cuts which would leave the other side at a disadvantage, and have therefore been rejected. On occasions, however, real opportunities have presented themselves, typically when the negotiators on one side have finally shifted their positions to coincide with the other side's proposals, only to see those be withdrawn. These missed opportunities are particularly saddening when the subsequent proliferation of weapons makes an eventual agreement more difficult to obtain. On some occasions progress is made, but negotiators then tend to find that they are moving more quickly than domestic political pressures will allow, and the process falters once more.

Many proposals have been made as to how disarmament negotiations might be made more productive. Some have argued that the answer lies in war prevention based on international security (Benjamin, 1983), have stressed the positive steps that can be taken as a consultant in peacemaking (Mitchell, 1981), the problem-solving workshop approach to the settling of disputes (Burton, 1979) or the changes in attitudes which will be required to turn from violent responses to peaceful attainment of common goals (Frank, 1982). One early approach will be discussed as an illustration, and because in different forms the ideas proposed have gained acceptance.

Osgood (1962) has proposed a negotiating approach called graduated reciprocation in tension reduction, which he sees as the alternative to the unacceptable duo of war or surrender. It is seen as a flexible interactive procedure in which each party regulates its own initiatives on the basis of the reciprocating actions taken by the other side. The aim is to reduce tension and create an atmosphere of mutual trust. Trust is not seen as a necessary precondition of talks, but as something which builds up as a consequence of unilateral moves. Such moves do not rule out multi-lateral negotiations, which are a natural part of the process. The rules which Osgood suggests need to be followed can be summarized briefly thus:

(i) Initiatives must not leave one side with a monopoly of nuclear weapons. The aim should be reductions, but the final steps will require bilateral agreement.

(ii) Initiatives must not cripple the capacity for conventional defence.

(iii) Initiatives should be graduated in risk according to the response. The first move must be fairly large and dramatic, and an immediate response should not be expected.

(iv) Initiatives must be diverse, publicly announced, and then carried through. Cultural as well as military issues could be included, the steps to be taken should be announced in advance, and then adhered to.

Etzioni (1967) carried out a study of arms negotiations between Kennedy and Kruschev between June and November 1963. He shows that a series of unilateral moves within carefully constrained limits were instrumental in bringing about bilateral agreements. Etzioni's account of these events is summarized as follows:

10th June. Although less than a year had elapsed since the Cuban missile crisis, Kennedy made a speech in which he called for a reappraisal of the Soviet Union in the light of constructive changes in that nation, and also asked Americans to re-examine their role in the Cold War. Kennedy then unilaterally announced an end to all atmospheric nuclear tests. (This move was less dramatic than it seemed. The US had just completed so many tests that the results would take two years to analyse. There was also domestic pressure to reduce radioactive contamination, and underground testing was allowed to continue.)

11th June. In the UN the USSR unilaterally removed its objections to Western observers in the Yemeni civil war. The US withdrew its opposition to full membership for Hungary, which it had opposed since 1956. The full text of Kennedy's speech was printed in Russian newspapers, and radio jammers taken off Voice of America broadcasts.

15th June. Kruschev welcomed Kennedy's speech, and recipro-cated the atmospheric test ban, and announced that, contrary to Marxist-Leninist doctrine, war was not inevitable between com-munism and capitalism. Kruschev unilaterally announced that the USSR would cease strategic bomber production. (This too was more apparent than real, since the decision had probably already been taken on military grounds, but it served to reciprocate peace initiatives.)

20th June. USSR agreed to an earlier US proposal, that a 'hot line' be established between the two nations. For the next few months negotiations continued on the Partial Test Ban Treaty, which was signed on 5th August.

9th October. Kennedy approved a $250 million wheat deal with the Soviet Union, which served as a psychological move, although other trade restrictions remained.

19th September. Gromyko suggested an agreement be reached prohibiting the orbiting of nuclear weapons in space. The US reciprocated this unilateral move, and the treaty was signed on 19th October.

By late October the process began to slow. Etzioni (1967) argues that the US became alarmed that the USSR was reciprocating so fast, and going one better, that it was beginning to control the process. NATO allies, particularly West Germany, began to protest, and as the election approached Kennedy felt that he had done enough for the time being, and that more moves would put him at risk politically of the accusation of appeasement. Kennedy's assassination brought an end to the process.

Crossley (1983) gives further accounts of circumstances in which limited unilateral initiatives have assisted the negotiation process.

In February 1971 US satellites revealed that the Russians were building alarmingly large new missile silos, putting the SALT process at risk. In April 1971, for the sole purpose of US satellites, Russian constructors laid out all the silo liners in sequence of insertion to show how they would be assembled, together with a missile container. In fact, all that had happened was that they had changed their construction methods. Instead of boring a narrow deep hole and fitting the liners down into it, they dug a wide funnel into the ground, assembled the liners, poured round some concrete, and then bulldozed the earth back in. What had changed was the apparent diameter of the hole during construction, and not the missile size.

Unilateral initiatives have been made by the Soviet Union in April 1971 by slowing down production of SS9 missiles, by revealing Warsaw Pact force levels in April 1975; by the United States in November 1969 renouncing bacteriological weapons, and promising no first use of lethal chemical weapons, and in April 1978 President Carter announcing no production of neutron bombs, Brezhnev reciprocating; and by the United Kingdom in June 1983 giving details of key chemical production in order to show that the chemicals were not being used for military purposes.

A first move by one party in a conflict, even if relatively small in itself, can have a psychological impact, which can then make later reciprocal moves more likely. The political terms 'multilateralism' and 'unilateralism' are not helpful in describing this process, since they are associated with polarized interpretations, with political overtones.

It would be more accurate and more productive if negotiation processes were studied in terms of a variety of measures. For example, each proposal could be studied in terms of the degree of risk to which it exposes each party, the perceived likelihood of falling within the other party's acceptable range, and the extent to which reciprocity is required. The common standards underlying these judgements would themselves require agreement. It will be seen that on this simple analysis, the proposal least likely to succeed is one that is perceived as risky, beyond the limits of acceptance, and requiring high reciprocity. Yet these are the usual ingredients of which many highly publicized disarmament proposals are composed. They tend to be rejected outright, or countered with proposals which are equally unacceptable to the other side. From a pure bargaining point of view, these may seem to be traditional ways in which to 'reconnoitre the range', but the psychological cost tends to be distrust and a highly competitive orientation. Proposals with a higher chance of success are those which are low in risk, within acceptance range, and make low demands on reciprocity. Immediate practical gains may be very small, but the cumulative psychological effect may be to build trust and engender a cooperative orientation.

Section 4. **Theory into practice**

A considerable difference in methodology and style exists between academic studies of conflict, and practical manuals for negotiators. While the full range of these cannot be discussed, an example can be taken to illustrate some attempts to offer practical suggestions. It is likely that such material can only offer some ideas, and that problem-solving workshops and training would be needed for practical competence (Burton, 1979).

Fisher and Ury (1981) have described in a clear and accessible form some of the work of the Harvard Negotiation Project, which seeks to move away from hard or soft positional bargaining towards what they call principled negotiation or negotiation on the merits. They vividly describe the futility of bargaining from entrenched positions and show that neither an adversorial, distrustful, threatening 'hard' posture nor a friendly, trustful, concessionary 'soft' posture will lead to satisfactory long-term results. Naturally a soft approach is likely to speed up agreement, but it may not be a wise one.

Principled negotiation can be summarized in four points.

1. People: Separate the people from the problem. The intention behind separating the people from the problem is to reduce the psychological identification with a position which can then lead to intransigence and face-saving. The idea is to build up a mood in which participants work side by side attacking the problem and not each other. Sherif (1962) has shown that only a common problem worked at on a cooperative basis is likely to change the antagonistic feelings of two competitive groups. Attempts at fraternization were unsuccessful, but joint activity to solve a problem which had equal impact on both groups brought about a considerable change in attitudes.

2. Interests: Focus on interests, not positions. Negotiating positions are often adopted to allow for later concessions, or to obscure the real desires of the participants. By concentrating on underlying interests rather than surface positions one is more likely to produce an agreement which meets the human needs which led to the adoption of the bargaining positions in the first place.

3. Options: Generate a variety of possibilities before deciding what to do. Trying to work out the best solution to a dispute under pressure facing an adversary can narrow vision and inhibit creativity. These constraints can be overcome by setting aside time within which to think up a wide range of possible solutions that advance shared interests and creatively reconcile differing interests. Before trying to reach agreement, one must invent options for mutual gain.

4. Criteria: Insist that the result be based on some objective standard. Stubborness can slow or distort the negotiation procedure, leading to arbitrary results as a consequence of naked will alone. A way out of this potential impasse is to agree a common objective standard, and then meet those criteria.

The communication process itself should proceed through the stages of analysis, planning and discussion, using the above four points as guidelines.

A further discussion of how to separate the people from the problem concentrates on problems of perception and communication. Fisher and Ury stress 'Ultimately, conflict lies not in objective reality but in people's heads.' They recommend the open discussion of perceptions, guarding against projecting malevolent intentions on the basis of fear. They also stress that without effective communication there can be no negotiation. Participants must listen actively and acknowledge what is being said. They must achieve understanding, not win debating points. Finally, emotions must be recognized and given some legitimate and non-destructive means of expression, or they will begin to determine the nature of the negotiation.

A case example: Camp David

Rogers (1984) presents personal experiences of being a facilitator at meetings of antagonistic or feuding groups, and recounts the general pattern of such encounters. Opposing groups are generally convinced of the righteousness of their cause, and the first task of the facilitator is to provide a nonjudgmental and accepting forum in which these views can be heard. In a sense the capacity to hear out and understand the opposing views makes it easier for the antagonistic parties to begin to hear and understand the concerns of the other side. An understanding atmosphere gives equality of expression to groups which may differ considerably in status, giving them temporary access to good communication. The facilitator does not persuade or take sides, but creates the psychological climate in which group wisdom can emerge. Taking the long-standing hatreds of Northern Ireland as an example, Rogers reports that even 16 hours of discussion between antagonistic groups was sufficient to soften hatreds, and in some instances deeply change them. The group continued to function on their return to Belfast, and showed the film of the group proceedings to church groups in the city. Key factors were that both factions had been removed from their own locale to a residential retreat setting and that an informal atmosphere was encouraged. A dangerous consequence of even this limited intervention was that the rapprochement of the group members put them into a vulnerable position when they returned home to their implacably opposed camps.

Rogers and Ryback (1984) then go on to comment on the Camp David experience as a psychological encounter. The September 1978 meeting shared the common features of a residential setting and an informal atmosphere. The accommodation was comfortable but not pretentious, and there was daily casual contact between the Israeli and Egyptian teams. There was no protocol, and people sat where they liked at mealtimes. Sadat and more particularly Begin retained formality of dress and manner most of the time. However, they were able to speak as people and not primarily as agents acting for their constituencies back at home.

The conference was self-contained and private, without media coverage. Wide exposure of the initial bargaining positions would have simply locked the protagonists into intransigence. In consultation with the Harvard Negotiation Project, a one-text procedure was followed, so that both sides worked to try to improve a single American draft, rather than battle over separate texts.

No agenda was set for the meetings nor were there regular working hours. The meetings themselves were often very emotional. Feelings ran high, and Carter reported: 'There was no compatability between the two men, and almost every discussion of any subject deteriorated into an unproductive argument, reopening the old wounds of past political or military battles' (Carter, p.355). Most of the participants lost their temper at some point, and failure seemed likely.

During some angry exchanges between Begin and Sadat, Carter said practically nothing but took extensive notes, which he read out to both of them at the end of the meeting, thus stating calmly and clearly the issues which had divided them, so that they could be seen in a more rational light. Tension was often broken by laughter, but when it was so high that the leaders refused to meet each other, Carter acted as a go-between. Rogers and Ryback note that it is rare for participants to refuse to meet each other for very long.

In Camp David, as in any intensive group, feelings became intensified, and the highs and lows were felt far more acutely because the conflicting parties were in contact every day with just one focus in mind. On separate occasions each of the three leaders thought that the meeting had failed. Sadat packed his bags on the eleventh day, and on the thirteenth and last day Begin decided he would not sign anything and that the conference was a failure.

Rogers states, but is unable to explain, that 'it has sometimes seemed to me that in intensive group sessions with hostile groups, it is only when I recognize that no progress can be made, that the cause is helpless, that somehow a turning point is reached'. In Rogers' view the incident which seems to have turned Camp David from a complete failure into a significant success was a highly personal one. Photographs of the three leaders together had been taken. Sadat had signed them, and Carter was about to also, since Begin had requested some for his three grandchildren. Carter's secretary, Susan Clough, suggested that he personalize the signatures with the children's names. He did this, and took them over to Begin. When he saw the names he became very emotional, and spoke with tears in his eyes about them. An hour later he phoned to

accept the new draft of the agreement on Jerusalem. He then visited
Sadat in his cabin and agreed some further points. Rogers comments:

> To some it may seem very strange that the turning point of an
> international conference of great significance was based on a tearful
> discussion of grandchildren, rather than the issues of the con-
> ference. Yet to us who have experienced intensive groups this seems
> quite natural. It is when the deepest personal feelings are touched
> that change takes place in the individual's attitude.

Naturally, whether these feelings continue depends on the situation and
the people involved.

On a more critical note, Rogers points out that the remaining 24
members of the delegation were not included in the intensive group
experience. They were unable to fully support their leaders' painfully
achieved new positions, since they had not experienced the intense
emotional interaction of the conference. Some of Sadat's delegates
resigned, and Begin met a storm of criticism on his return home. A
failure to consider these matters can often render peacemakers vulnerable.

Section 5. **New approaches to nuclear negotiations**

Having discussed some ways in which negotiations can be improved,
these approaches can now be applied to the nuclear case.

The Harvard Nuclear Negotiation Project (Ury and Smoke, 1984) is
attempting to find more effective methods of defusing a crisis than those
available in the simple hotline procedures. Ury and Smoke share the
view that the most likely path to nuclear war is through miscalculation,
miscommunication or accident, and that with nuclear proliferation and
the prospect of nuclear terrorism the possibilities of such errors
continue to rise. They list the four key characteristics of a crisis that
make it difficult to control: little time to decide, high stakes, high
uncertainty and few usable options. To counter these problems steps
must be taken in advance to ensure that there is time for each side to
make wise decisions, that the stakes are kept under control, that
uncertainty is reduced and that each side is left acceptable ways out of
the crisis. The emphasis is always on the preparatory work needed in
order that an eventual crisis should be survivable.

Ury and Smoke came to these draft proposals by questioning
American policy makers about crisis management, getting them to
imagine they were at the beginning of a serious crisis and then asking
them what they wished they had discussed with the Soviets beforehand,

and what joint institutional arrangements they might have wished they had in place. On the basis of these discussions Ury and Smoke give six specific measures for crisis control and avoidance.

(i) Further agreed-upon crisis procedures

The 'Hotline' and the 1972 'Incidents at Sea' agreement are procedures which could be extended to include accidental ground and air intrusions and to provide a means of coping with nuclear detonations whose source and motive are unclear. Six such arrangements have already been formalized, of which the 1963 hotline is the best known. Some of the above points were contained in the Nunn-Jackson proposal of September 1982, which also proposed improvements in verification procedures and measures to lengthen the warning time both nations would have of possible attack.

The Accidents Agreement of 1971 already commits each side to notify the other about unauthorized launchings and any events that could be dangerously misinterpreted. Agreements of this sort serve as a very useful beginning in what could be a much larger process of mutual agreement on measures for jointly coping with possible nuclear crises.

(ii) Nuclear crisis control centre

Joint US–Soviet facilities in Washington and Moscow, connected by instant teleconferencing, at which diplomats and military officers would continuously monitor potential crises and help prevent inadvertent war. Such a centre could help deal with the tension which arises from unintended ground and air incursions, as well as conflicts arising from third party wars. The centre would be composed of a small group of Russian and American defence and diplomatic experts. In normal times they would work to devise possible crisis prevention and control measures for a range of possible contingencies. In times of crisis the centre could facilitate the exchange and validation of information, help implement agreed-upon procedures and be a problem-solving resource to aid other decision-makers.

(iii) Crisis consultation period

A declaratory or agreed-upon delay for reflection and consultation following one or a few nuclear detonations on one's territory in order to ascertain origin and intentions before making a retaliatory strike. In the early 'sixties Secretary of Defense McNamara urged that the US adopt such a policy, and repeated his proposal in 1983, saying that no retaliatory second strike should be made 'until it has been determined beyond any possible doubt that the nuclear explosion to which the second use responds was in fact intentional and purposeful' (*New York Times*, 1983). Such a policy would be a considerable help in knowing how best to respond to nuclear terrorism by third parties.

(iv) Nuclear risk reduction talks

Semi-annual meetings between Soviet and American defence and foreign secretaries so as to review progress and develop new consultative mechanisms.

(v) Crisis control seminars

A proposed briefing and 'crisis exercise' to acquaint a President or President-elect with crisis management. Ury and Smoke point out that Presidents receive some exposure to war games, but very little to crisis control procedures. Although this proposal is directed toward the American side, a crisis centre team should be able to provide such information to either side.

(vi) Enhanced third-party roles in defusing regional conflicts

Superpower support for mediation and peacekeeping forces in regional conflicts which might otherwise draw the superpowers into an unwanted and dangerous confrontation.

From a psychological point of view it is interesting to note that Ury and Smoke identify very similar factors to those found by other researchers in crisis management. The detailed nature of their proposals, and their access to crisis participants for advice as to what procedures need to be established or extended, makes their work of particular importance in the field of crisis control.

Some practical suggestions: a reflection on the research evidence

On the basis of findings from previous crises, can any psychological advice be given with a view to avoiding a future nuclear confrontation? The tentative answer seems to be that preventative steps must be taken long before a crisis takes place, since crises establish their own momentum, so the following points are raised with a view to creating better relations in the long term. They are based on the observations and suggestions of psychologists who have studied the field.

Governments and their publics are often out of step, since governmental political rhetoric may be believed, and profoundly influence public perception of other nations long after the government itself has followed less-publicized courses of action to secure its own interests. Thus both Soviet and American governments may have highly critical public postures while privately agreeing on trade deals and the containment of third party conflicts. Public reactions may often prevent a government from changing course as soon as it would wish. Therefore, if changes are to occur, they must be coordinated to occur at both the public and the governmental level.

(i) Symbolic changes

At a time of tension and fear, symbolic moves may be all that nations dare make. At the same time, distrust may make the competitive parties unwilling to make even symbolic concessions. Normalization of relations allows the everyday interplay of trade, tourism and cultural exchange to proceed, and although such communication does not have immediate effects, it acts as the lubricating oil of international relations. Economic and political sanctions rarely achieve their ends, and serve only to distort perceptions. Normal relations are not a prize to be achieved at the end of negotiations: they are almost one of the prior conditions. Any steps taken to normalize relations will bring better communication, more room to manoeuvre, and a public more willing to support initiatives in international relations.

(ii) Rhetoric

Hostile speeches inflame emotions, spread fear and distrust, and restrict freedom of manoeuvre in negotiations. They may sustain a politician with a home audience, but they damage relations with the larger audience who hear themselves slandered. It would be helpful if political leaders were always to speak of the other side as if they were present at their dinner tables.

(iii) Personal contacts and communication

It is common knowledge in the business world that the act of faith involved in entering into any contract or agreement is considerably assisted by having personal knowledge of the people involved. To this end businessmen meet, chat and eat together in order to gain the wider knowledge about each other which formal settings cannot provide. Personal knowledge assists negotiation, and is an important source of business. By contrast, political leaders have relatively little contact across the East–West divide, and have little chance of informal contact to learn about each other's style of thinking. American politicians involved in the Cuban missile crisis stated that their greatest problem was not knowing the other side well enough to know how they would react to their actions. Problem-solving workshops (Burton, 1979; Rogers, 1984) with the 'middle management' of the superpowers, carried out over a period of years could be the greatest single factor in improving the negotiating process. Some first steps are already being taken in this direction (Ury, 1984).

(iv) Responding to proposals

The hasty rejection of the other side's disarmament proposals is one aspect of the propaganda war. A better psychological approach would be to welcome any proposal, and to discuss the shortcomings only in private, together with suggestions for improvement. Even better would be to attempt to use a private single text procedure (Fisher and Ury, 1981) so that both parties work to improve a joint proposal which can then be made public.

(v) Delayed effect agreements

At times of tension, weapons appear to confer security. Therefore, it is easier to attempt to reach agreement on matters which have more distant effects. This would fit in with the theory of graduated tension reduction (Osgood, 1962). A total nuclear test ban has been almost within the grasp of the superpowers for 20 years. Verification is now a much simpler matter than before (Institute of Seismology, 1984), and such a ban would have a delayed restraining effect on the pace of weapons development, as well as serving as a model of verified arms control.

(vi) Crisis and accident prevention

The hotline must be expanded, and necessary institutions created to act effectively and promptly when crises threaten to occur (Ury and Smoke, 1984). This work will take time, and steps taken once a crisis has occurred have less chance of success. Accident prevention is clearly in the common interest of both parties, and could serve a starting point for extensive discussions.

(vii) Categorization of negotiations

The present separation of negotiations into contentious and overlapping categories has worsened the psychological mood in which discussions take place. Counting weapons has always been an emotionally fraught procedure, and the present arrangements have made it worse. It would probably be better to unify the discussions around interests rather than positions or weapons systems. For example, a central interest of both parties is to have time to decide what to do in a crisis. Possibly negotiations about signalling intentions and avoiding command centre attacks might have more to contribute to the disarmament process at this stage than cuts in weapons numbers (Ury and Smoke, 1984; Bracken, 1984).

(viii) Common tasks and objectives

Great political, social and financial forces maintain the arms race within both superpowers. These forces make it difficult for changes to be made, and new tasks will have to be found if energies are to be redirected. The international military-industrial-political complex is the joint creation of Soviet–American enterprise, and the weight of institutional planning and power is effectively on the side of continuing superpower conflict. Many options will have to be created and discussed so that resources can be directed to new enterprises. The benefits of redirecting military expenditure to social needs would be considerable (Sivard, 1983), but most nations do not feel confident enough to do so.

Remaining difficulties

For negotiations to succeed, the motivation to achieve a solution must overcome the motivation to seek maximum advantage. The US and the USSR have reportedly had over 6000 official meetings since the end of the Second World War, and the nuclear stockpiles of both nations have shown a continual increase.

One example of this approach has been made public. Richard Burt, Assistant Secretary of State for European Affairs, said of the current arms talks: 'The purpose of this whole exercise is maximum political advantage. It's not arms control we're engaged in, it's alliance management' (*Time*, 1983, no 49). Such an attitude in either party at a negotiation severely reduces the chance of agreement.

Faced with a conflict between the apparent high probability of being attacked by the other side if they gain an advantage in the arms race, and the apparently lower probability of both sides being destroyed when the race culminates in a war, both sides have chosen to continue the race. They have effectively seen their relationship as a zero-sum game, in which any influence or power gained by one side will be lost by the other. The challenge is to turn the relationship into a positive-sum game, in which the benefits of cooperation are seen to outweigh the supposed advantages of continued competition.

At present each side adds weapons in the way that a herdsman adds animals to a herd. Each additional weapon adds the benefit of apparent security in the way that each additional animal adds the benefit of increased productivity. There is a cost, but that cost is deferred and shared by all society. The cost in the case of the herdsman is the depletion of the earth's limited resources through overgrazing. In the case of the arms race, the cost is the depletion of human and natural resources, plus the ever-present risk of nuclear destruction. Hardin (1968) argued that as a result of population growth modern humanity faced a problem analogous to that faced by herdsmen using a common pasture. Each herdsman realizes that an additional animal brings him benefit while the cost must be shared by everyone.

> Therein is the tragedy. Each man is locked into a system that compels him to increase his herd without limit - in a world that is limited. Ruin is the destination toward which all men rush, each pursuing his own best interest in a society that believes in the freedom of the commons. (p.1244)

Eventually the joint costs of individual actions become known, and on the basis of such knowledge, and in the face of an immediate perceived threat, corrective action can be attempted. Time to reflect on the full impact of a personal choice has been shown to increase socially co-operative decisions in simulated social dilemmas (Marwell and Ames, 1979), but where the threat may not be perceived until it is too late, such reflection may not be possible.

Summary and conclusions

International crises are composed of many factors, but although historical, cultural and social factors will play their part, the psychological component will always remain. Particularly at times of crisis, decision-making becomes concentrated in a small number of people, and their psychological makeup takes on a disproportionate importance. Their view of the world, their nation and what they believe to be 'the lessons of history' have an important bearing on the decisions they make. As crises begin, the participants are put under increasing pressure. The increased emotional and information-processing demands begin to take their toll. Perceptions become polarized into simple opposing categories, and the options for problem solution appear to become severely limited. The stress of decision-making leads to a strong need for support and unity, and independent critical advice may be ignored because it questions cherished assumptions. The pressure of time has a strong effect on crisis management, and can lead to decisions which make the crisis worse. Group pressures may take over the crisis participants, so that they begin to act in ways which they later find hard to explain. These factors, taken together with the shorter decision times imposed by modern weapons systems, signify that crisis decision-making in a nuclear age is inevitably highly risky, and represents a substantial danger.

A comparison of superpower crisis management techniques shows some differences between the superpowers, and reveals that violence has often led to the achievement of their national goals.

The main hope of crisis prevention lies in improving negotiations, and thus making crises far less common. Although psychological techniques cannot easily overcome historical and cultural factors, they can make a contribution to conflict resolution. Much of the work done in negotiations lies in gaining a proper understanding of the world picture held by each party, and understanding the interests which underlie public negotiating positions. Bargaining can easily become locked into a spiral of distrust, and problem-solving workshops offer an example of a way out of this impasse. A variety of psychological techniques exist for breaking down antagonistic postures, and getting opposing parties to work together for mutual gain. Far more use could be made of these techniques than is apparent from current disarmament negotiations.

REFERENCES

Akizuki, T. (1981) *Nagasaki 1945*. London: Quartet.
Albrecht, U., Asbjorn, E., Kaldor, M., Leitenberg, M. and Robinson, J.P. (1978) *A Short Research Guide on Arms and Armed Forces*. London: Croom Helm.
Alexandrov, V.V. and Stenchikov, G.L. (1983) *On the modelling of the climactic consequences of the nuclear war*. Paper published by The Computing Centre of the USSR Academy of Sciences.
AMBIO (1983) *Nuclear War: The Aftermath*. Stockholm: Royal Swedish Academy of Sciences/Oxford: Pergamon Press.
Anderson, E.W. (1942) Psychiatric syndrome following blast. *Journal of Mental Science*, **88**, 328.
Andren, N. (1981) Future studies and national security: the Swedish experience. *Nordic Journal of International Politics*, **16**,(1).
Arbours, A.G. and Karrick, J.E. (1951) Accident statistics and the concept of accident-proneness. *Journal of the Biometric Society*, **7**, 340-429.
Archibald, H.C.D., Long, D.M., Miller, C. and Tuddenham, R.D. (1963) Gross stress reactions in combat. *American Journal of Psychiatry*, **119**, 317.
Asch, S. (1956) Studies of independence and conformity: 1. A minority of one against a unanimous majority. *Psychological Monographs*, **70**.
Axelrod, R. (1976) *The Structure of Decision*. Princeton: Princeton University Press.
Bachman, G.G. (in press) How American high school seniors view the military. *Armed Forces and Society*.
Barnaby, F. (1981) Military-Scientists. *Bulletin of the Atomic Scientists*, **37**(6), 11–12.
Beardslee, W. and Mack, J. (1982) The impact on children and adolescents of nuclear developments. *American Psychiatric Association Task Force Report No. 20: Psychosocial aspects of nuclear developments*. Washington DC: American Psychiatric Association.
Benjamin, R. (1983) Relations between disarmament and world secur-

ity. Paper presented at the Second Conference of Professions for World Disarmament and Development, London.

Bennett, P.G. and Dando, M.R. (1983) The arms race: is it just a mistake? *New Scientist*, **17 Feb**, 432–435.

Bereanu, B. (1983) Self-activation of the world nuclear weapons system. *Journal of Peace Research*, **20**, 49–57.

Beres, L. (1980) *Apocalypse: Nuclear Catastrophe in World Politics.* Chicago: University of Chicago Press.

Betts, R.K. (1977) *Soldiers, Statesmen and Cold War Crises.* Cambridge, Mass.: Harvard University Press.

Beussee, M.P., Ahearn, T.R. and Hammes, J.A. (1970) Introspective reports of large groups experimentally confined in an austere environment. *Journal of Clinical Psychology*, **26**, 240–244.

Borning, A. (1984) Computer system reliability and nuclear war. Paper presented at the International Physicians for the Prevention of Nuclear War 4th Congress in Helsinki, June 1984.

Bracken, P. (1983) *The Command and Control of Nuclear Weapons.* New Haven, Conn.: Yale University Press.

Brassey's Publishers (1982) *Nuclear Attack: Civil Defence.* London: Royal United Services Institute for Defence Studies.

Bray, R.M., Guess, L.L., Mason, R.E., Hubbard, R.L., Smith, D.G., Marsden, M.E. and Rachal, J. (1983) *Highlights: 1982 worldwide survey of alcohol and nonmedical drug use among military personnel.* Research Triangle Institute Report, RTI/2317/01/01F July 1983.

Brecher, M. (1978) *Studies in Crisis Behaviour.* New Brunswick: Transaction Books.

Brill, N. and Beebe, G. (1955) *A follow up study of war neuroses. V.A. Med. Mono.* Washington DC: US Govt. Printing Office.

British Medical Association (1983) *The Medical Effects of Nuclear War.* Chichester: Wiley.

Britten, S. (1983) *The Invisible Event: An Assessment of the Risk of Accidental or Unauthorized Detonation of Nuclear Weapons and of War by Miscalculation.* London: Menard Press.

Bromet, E. (1980) *Three Mile Island: Mental Health Findings.* Pittsburgh, Penn.: Western Psychiatric Institute and Clinic, University of Pittsburgh.

Bronfenbrenner, U. (1961) The mirror-image in Soviet–American relations – a social psychologist's report. *Journal of Social Issues*, **17**, 45–56.

Brown, G.W., Harris, T.O. and Peto, J. (1973) Life events and psychiatric disorders: nature of the causal link. *Psychological Medicine*, **3**, 159.

Burt, M. (1980) Prevalence and consequences of drug abuse among US military personnel: 1980. *American Journal of Drug and Alcohol Abuse*, **8**, 419–437.

Burton, J. (1979) *Deviance, Terrorism and War*. Oxford: Martin Robertson.

Business Decisions (1983) *Nuclear weapons study – summary report*. Survey conducted for the *TV Times*.

Campbell, D. (1983) *War Plan UK*. St Albans: Palladin.

Campbell, D.T. (1958) Systematic error on the part of human links in communication systems. *Information and Control*, **1**, 334–369.

Canter, D. and Powell, J. (1983) *Summary of report to Insurance Technical Bureau*. Guildford: University of Surrey.

Carter, J. (1982) *Keeping Faith*. New York: Bantam.

Casscells, W., Schoenberger, A. and Graboys, T.B. (1978) Interpretation by physicians of clinical laboratory results. *The New England Journal of Medicine*, **299**, 999–1001.

Central Intelligence Agency (1976) *International and Transnational Terrorism*.

Central Office of Information (1980) *Protect and Survive*. London: HMSO.

Chazov, E.I. and Vartanian, M.E. (1983) Effects on human behaviour. In: AMBIO *Nuclear War: The Aftermath*. Stockholm: Royal Swedish Academy of Sciences/Oxford: Pergamon Press.

Cherns, A.B. (1962) Accidents at work. In: Welford, A.T., Argyle, M., Glass, D.V. and Morris, J.W. (eds) *Society: Problems and Methods of Study*. London: Routledge and Kegan Paul.

Childs, D. (1983) Personal communication. Letter of July 1983.

Chivian, E. (1983) Adverse effects on children. In: Farrow, S. and Chown, A. (eds) *The Human Cost of Nuclear War*. Cardiff: Medical Campaign against Nuclear Weapons/Titan Press.

Churcher, J., Gleisner, J., Lieven, E. and Pushkin, R. (1981) Nuclear war and civil defence: some psychological and social implications. Paper presented at The British Psychological Society Annual Conference, 1981.

Churcher, J. and Lieven, E. (1983) Images of nuclear war and the public in British civil defence. *Journal of Social Issues*, **39**, 117.

Cleveland, S.E., Boyd, I., Sheer, D. and Reitman, E.E. (1963) Effects of fallout shelter confinement on family adjustment. *Archives of General Psychiatry*, **8**, 38–46.

Cobb, S. and Lindemann, E. (1944) Neuropsychiatric observations during the Coconut Grove Fire. *Annals of Surgery*, **117**, 814.

Colquhoun, W.P. (1971) *Biological Rhythms and Human Performance*.

London: Academic Press.

Colquhoun, W.P. (1975) Effects of circadian rhythm, sleep deprivation, and fatigue on watchkeeping performance during the night hours. In: Colquhoun, W.P., Folkard, S., Knauth, P. and Rutenfanz, J. (eds) *Experimental Studies of Shiftwork.* Opladen: West Deutscher Verlag.

Colquhoun, W.P., Paine, M. and Fort, A., (1978) Circadian rhythms of body temperature during prolonged undersea voyages. *Aviation Space and Environmental Medicine,* **May 1978.**

Comey, D.D. (1975) How we almost lost Alabama. *Chicago Tribune,* **31 Aug,** *2.*

Congressional Record. House Committee on Appropriations. Subcommittee on Military Construction. (95th Congress, 2nd Session.) *Hearings on Military Construction Appropriations for 1979.*

Congressional Record. Hearings before the Select Committee on Narcotics Abuse and Control. House of Representatives. (97th Congress, 1st Session.) 17 September, 1981

Crossley, G.J. (in press) Unilateral initiatives: A route to safer international relations.

Crutzen, P.J and Birks, J.W. (1983) The atmosphere after a nuclear war: twilight at noon. In: AMBIO *Nuclear War: The Aftermath.* Stockholm: Royal Swedish Academy of Sciences/Oxford: Pergamon Press.

Cull, C., Erskine, A., Haug, U., Roper-Hall, A. and Thompson, J. (1983) Human fallibility in the control of nuclear weapons. In: Farrow, S. and Chown, A. (eds) *The Human Cost of Nuclear War.* Cardiff: Medical Campaign against Nuclear Weapons/Titan Press.

Dawes, R.M. (1980) Social dilemmas. *Annual Review of Psychology,* **31,** 169–193.

Defence Monitor (1981), 10(5). Washington DC: Centre for Defense Information.

Deutsch, M. (1958) Trust and suspicion. *Journal of Conflict Resolution,* **2,** 265–279

Deutsch, M. (1983) The prevention of World War III: a psychological perspective. Presidential address to the fifth annual meeting of the International Society for Political Psychology, Washington DC, June 26 1982. *Political Psychology,* **4,** 3–31.

Dixon, N.F. (1976) *On the Psychology of Military Incompetence.* London: Cape.

Dixon, N.F. (1983) The illusion of rational decision making. Paper presented at International Physicians for the Prevention of Nuclear War, 3rd Congress, Amsterdam.

Douglas, A. (1957) The peaceful settlement of industrial and intergroup disputes. *Journal of Conflict Resolution,* **1,** 69–81.

Douglas, A. (1962) *Industrial Peacemaking*. New York: Columbia University Press.

Dowie, J. and Lefrere, P. (eds) (1980) *Risk and Chance*. Milton Keynes: Open University Press.

Dumas, L.J. (1980) Human fallibility and weapons. *The Bulletin of the Atomic Scientists*, 15-20.

Dumas, L.J. (1982) Human and technical fallibility in military organizations. Paper presented at International Physicians for Prevention of Nuclear War, 3rd Congress, Amsterdam.

Eberwein, W.D. (1981) The quantitative study of international conflict: Quantity and quality? An assessment of empirical research. *Journal of Peace Research*, **18**, 19-38.

Eddy, D.M. (1982) Probabilistic reasoning in clinical medicine: Problems and opportunities. In: Kahneman, D., Slovic, P. and Tversky, A. (1982) *Judgement under Uncertainty: Heuristics and Biases*. Cambridge, Mass.: Cambridge University Press.

Edwards, J.G. (1976) Psychiatric aspects of civilian disasters. *British Medical Journal*, **17 April**, 944-947.

Eiser, J.R.and Van der Plight, J. (1979) Belief and values in the nuclear debate. *Journal of Applied Social Psychology*, **9**, 524-536.

Erikson, J. (1976) Loss of communality at Buffalo Creek. *American Journal of Psychiatry*, **133**, 302.

Escalona, S.K. (1963) Children's responses to the nuclear war threat. *Children*, **10**, 137-142.

Escalona, S.K. (1965) Children and the threat of nuclear war. In: Schwebel, M. (ed.) *Behavioural Science and Human Survival*. California: Behavioural Science Press.

Escalona, S.K. (1982) Growing up with the threat of nuclear war: Some indirect effects on personality development. *American Journal of Orthopsychiatry*, **52**, 600-607.

Etzioni, A. (1967) The Kennedy experiment. *Western Political Quarterly*, **20**, 361-380.

Feshbach, M. (1982) Between the lines of the 1979 Soviet census. *Problems of Communism*, **Jan-Feb.**

Festinger, R.L. (1957) *A Theory of Cognitive Dissonance*. Illinois: Row, Peterson.

Fischoff, B., Slovic, P. and Lichtenstein, S. (1978) Fault trees: Sensitivity of estimated failure probabilities to problem representation. *Journal of Experimental Psychology: Human Perception and Performance*, **4**, 342-355.

Fischoff, S.P. (1972) Effects of ego involvement, prenegotiation experience and reference group influence on outcomes in an experimental simulation of inter-group negotiation. *Dissertation Abstracts International*, **33(5-A)**, 2494.

Fisher, R. (1969) *International Conflict for Beginners*. London: Harper and Row.

Fisher, R. and Ury, W. (1981) *Getting to Yes*. London: Hutchinson.

Flynn, C.B. and Chalmers, J.A. (1980) *The social and economic effects of the accident at Three Mile Island: Findings to date*. NUREG CR, 1215. Washington DC: US Government Printing Office.

Frank, J. (1982) Pre-nuclear age leaders and the nuclear arms race. *American Journal of Orthopsychiatry*, **52**, 630–637.

Frei, D. (1983) *Risks of Unintentional Nuclear War*. London: Croom Helm.

Friedsam, H.J. (1962) Older persons in disaster. In: Baker, G.W. and Chapman, D.W. (eds) *Man and Society in Disaster*. New York: Basic Books.

Gallup Poll (1972) *Public Opinion 1959–1971, Vol III*. New York: Random House.

Glass, A.J. (1959) Psychological aspects of disaster. *Journal of the American Medical Association*, **171**, 222.

Glasstone, S. and Dolan, P.J. (1980) *The Effects of Nuclear Weapons*. Castle House, Tunbridge Wells: US Dept of Defense and US Dept of Energy.

Gorer, G. (1965) *Death, Grief and Mourning in Contemporary Britain*. London: Cresset.

Green, E.A. (1982) *High Risk Safety Technology*. Chichester: Wiley.

Gunter, B. and Wober, M. (1982) *Television viewing and public perceptions of hazards to life*. Report of the Independent Broadcasting Authority.

Halloran, R. (1982) Pentagon draws up first strategy for fighting a long nuclear war. *New York Times*, **30 May.**

Hardin, G.R. (1968) The tragedy of the commons. *Science*, **162**, 1243–1248.

Hansard (1984) Written answers. **14 March,** p.170.

Hermann, C.F. (1972) *International Crises: Insights from Behavioural Research*. New York: Free Press.

Hildebrandt, G. (1974) Circadian rhythms in different functions. In: Colquhoun, W.P., Folkard, S., Knauth, P. and Rutenfanz, J. (eds) (1975) *Experimental Studies of Shiftwork*. Opladen: West Deutscher Verlag.

Hindmarsh, I. (1980) Psychomotor function and psychoactive drugs. *British Journal of Clinical Pharmacology*, **10**, 189–209.

Hocking, F. (1965) Human reactions to extreme environmental stress.

Medical Journal of Australia, **2,** 477.

Holsti, D.R. (1972) Time, alternatives and communications: The 1914 and Cuban missile crises. In: Hermann, C.F. (ed.) *International Crises: Insights from Behavioural Research.* New York: Free Press.

Institute of Seismology (1984) Paper presented at the International Physicians for the Prevention of Nuclear War 4th Congress, Helsinki, Finland.

International Physicians for the Prevention of Nuclear War (1983) Medical articles on nuclear war. Papers presented at 3rd Congress Amsterdam.

Janis, I.L. (1971) *Stress and Frustration.* New York: Harcourt Brace.

Janis, I.L. (1972) *Victims of Group Think.* Boston: Houghton Mifflin.

Kabanov M.M. (1983) Personal communication. Symposium on problems of rational decision making. International Physicians for the Prevention of Nuclear War 3rd Congress, Amsterdam.

Kahneman, D., Slovic, P. and Tversky, A. (1982) *Judgement under Uncertainty: Heuristics and Biases.* Cambridge, Mass.: Cambridge University Press.

Katz, A.M. (1982) *Life after Nuclear War: The Economic and Social Impacts of Nuclear Attacks on the United States.* Cambridge, Mass.: Ballinger.

Kemeny, J. (1979) *The need for change: The legacy of TMI.* Report of the President's Commision on the accident at Three Mile Island. Washington DC: US Government Printing Office.

Kennedy, R.F. (1969) *13 Days.* London: Macmillan.

Kentsmith, D.K. (1980) Minimizing the psychological effects of a wartime disaster on an individual. *Aviation, Space and Environment Medicine*, **51,** 409–413.

Killian, L.M. (1952) The significance of multiple group membership in disaster. *American Journal of Sociology*, **57**(4), 310.

Kinston, W. and Rosser, R. (1974) Disaster: effects on mental and physical state. *Journal of Psychosomatic Research*, **18,** 437–456.

Koegler, R.R. and Hicks, S.M. (1972) The destruction of a medical centre by earthquake. *California Medicine*, **116,** 63.

Kubzansky, P.E. (1961) The effects of reduced environmental stimulation on human behaviour: a review. In: Biderman, A.D. and Zimmer, H. (eds) *The Manipulation of Human Behaviour.* New York: Wiley.

Lacey, G.N. (1972) Observations on Abervan. *Journal of Psychosomatic Research*, **16,** 257.

Lachman, R., Tatsuoka, M. and Bank, W.J. (1961) Human behaviour during the tsunami of May 1960. *Science,* **133,** 1405.

Laszlo, E. and Keys, D. (eds) (1981) *Disarmament: the Human Factor.* Oxford: Pergamon Press.

Lee, T.R. (1981) Perception of risk: the public's perception of risk and the question of irrationality. *Proceedings of the Royal Society, London,* **A376,** 5-16.

Lee, T.R., Brown, J. and Henderson, J. (1984) The psychology of nuclear anxiety. In: Surrey, J. (ed.) *The Urban Transportation of Irradiated Fuel.* London: Macmillan.

Leitenberg, M. (1978) *Arms control and disarmament: A short review of a thirty year history; and its impact on nuclear proliferation.* Discussion Paper issued by The Norman Patterson School of International Affairs, Carleton University, Ottawa, Canada.

Leitenberg, M. (1981) Presidential directive (PD) 59: United States nuclear weapon targeting policy. *Journal of Peace Research,* **28,** 309-317.

Levi A. (1981) Escalating commitment and risk taking in dynamic decision behaviour. Paper presented at the 89th Annual Convention of the American Psychological Association, Los Angeles.

Lievesley, S. (1979) A study of disasters and the welfare planning response in Australia and the UK. Unpublished PhD thesis, University of London.

Lifton, R.J. (1963) Psychological effects of the atomic bomb in Hiroshima: The theme of death. *Daedalus, Journal of the American Academy of Arts and Sciences,* **93,** (3).

Lifton, R.J. (1967) *Death in Life: Survivors of Hiroshima.* New York: Random House.

Lifton, R.J. and Olsen, E. (1976) Human meaning of total disaster. The Buffalo Creek experience. *Psychiatry,* **39,** 1-18.

Lindop, P.J. and Rotblatt, J. (1982) The consequences of radioactive fallout. In: Chivian, E., Chivian, S., Lifton, R.J. and Mack.J. (eds) *Last Aid: The Medical Dimensions of Nuclear War.* San Fransisco: Freeman.

Louche, C. (1975) The preparation of a group negotiation and its effects on the behaviour of the negotiators and their attitudes. *Bulletin de Psychologie,* **28,** 113-117.

Marris, P. (1974) *Loss and Change.* London: Routledge and Kegan Paul.

Marwell, G. and Ames, R.E. (1979) Experiments on the provision of public goods I: resources, interest, group size and the free rider problem. *American Journal of Sociology,* **84,** 1335-1360.

Meister, D. (1977) Methods of predicting human reliability in man-machine systems. In: Brown, S. and Martin, J. (eds) *Human Aspects of Man-Machine Systems.* Milton Keynes: Open University Press.

Menczer, L.F. (1968) The Hartford Disaster Exercise. *New England Journal of Medicine*, **278**, 822.

Milburn, T.W., Stewart, P.D. and Herman, R.K. (1982) A comparison of US and Soviet perceptions of one another's intentions. Cited Deutsch, M. (1982) *op. cit.*

Milgram, S. (1974) *Obedience to Authority*. London: Tavistock.

Mitchell, C.R. (1981) *Peacemaking and the Consultant's Role*. London: Gower.

Morley, I.E. (1979) Behavioural studies of industrial bargaining. In: Stephenson, G.M. and Brotherton, C.J. (eds) *Industrial Relations: A social-psychological approach*. Chichester: Wiley.

Morley, I.E. and Stevenson, G.M. (1977) *The Social Psychology of Bargaining*. London: Allen and Unwin.

Office of Technology Assessment, Congress of the United States (1980) *The Effects of Nuclear War*. London: Croom Helm.

Office of Technology Assessment, Congress of the United States (1981) *MX Missile Basing*. Washington DC: US Government Printing Office.

Oppenheim, A.N. (1984) Psychological perspectives in conflict research. In: Banks, M. (ed.) *Conflict in World Society*. London: Wheatsheaf Books.

Openshaw, S., Steadman, P. and Green, O. (1983) *Doomsday: Britain after a nuclear attack*. Oxford: Blackwell.

Osgood, C.E. (1962) *An Alternative to War or Surrender*. Urbana: University of Illinois Press.

Oskamp, S. (1965) Attitudes toward US and Russian actions: A double standard. *Psychological Reports*, **16**, 43–46.

Paige, G.D. (1972) Comparative case analysis of crisis decisions: Korea and Cuba. In: Mermann, C.F. (ed.) *International Crises: Insights from behavioural research*. New York: Free Press.

Parker, G. (1977) Cyclone Tracy and the Darwin evacuees, on the restoration of species. *British Journal of Psychiatry*, **130**, 548–555.

Parkes, C.M. (1965) Bereavement and mental illness. *British Journal of Medical Psychology*, **38**(1), 1.

Peace Action West (1982) *Target Wiltshire*. Bradford on Avon: Peace Action West.

Perrow, C. (1984) *Normal Accidents: Living with High-Risk Technologies*. New York: Basic Books.

Petrov, V.N. (1983) Changes in ozone content from a nuclear explosion. In: Chivian, E., Chivian, S., Lifton, R.J. and Mack, J. (eds) *Last Aid*. San Fransisco: Freeman.

Popovic, M. and Petrovic, D. (1964) After the Earthquake. *Lancet*, **2**,

1169.

Presidential Commission on the Accident at Three Mile Island, *Report*, **(1979)** Washington DC: US Government Printing Office.

Prins, G. (ed.) (1983) *Defended to Death*. Harmondsworth: Penguin Books.

Quarantelli, E.L. (1954) The nature and conditions of panic. *American Journal of Sociology*, **60**, 267.

Rangell, L. (1976) Discussion of the Buffalo Creek disaster: The course of psychic trauma. *American Journal of Psychiatry*, **133**, 313.

Reason, J. (1982) *Absent-minded?* New Jersey: Prentice-Hall.

Rogers, C.R. and Ryback, D. (1984) One alternative to nuclear planetary suicide. Private circulation by first author of two related papers.

Royal Society (1983) *Risk Assessment – A study group report*. London: Royal Society.

Rubin, J.Z. (1981) Psychological traps. *Psychology Today*, **15**, 52–63.

Rusk, Dean (1984) Some practical and realistic advice. *Time magazine*, **No. 1**, 2 Jan, 22.

Russell, B. (1927) *Philosophy*. New York: Norton.

Rutter, M. (1981) Stress, coping and development: some issues and some questions. *Journal of Child Psychology and Psychiatry*, **22**, 323–356.

Schwebel, M. (1982) Effects of the nuclear threat on children and teenagers: Implications for professionals. *American Journal of Orthopsychiatry*, **52**, 608–618.

Seligman, M.P. (1975) *Helplessness: On depression, development and death*. San Francisco: Freeman.

Sherif, M. (1962) *Intergroup Relations and Leadership*. New York: Wiley.

Simon, H. (1983) *Reason in Human Affairs*. Oxford: Blackwell.

Sivard, R.L. (1983) *World Military and Social Expenditures*. Washington DC: World Priorities.

Slovic, P. and Fischoff, B. (1980) How safe is safe enough? In: Dowie, J. and Lefrere, P. (eds) *Risk and Chance*. Milton Keynes: Open University Press.

Slovic, P., Fischoff, B. and Lichtenstein, S. (1982) Facts versus fears: understanding perceived risk. In: Kahneman, D., Slovic, P. and Tversky, A. (eds) *Judgement under Uncertainty: Heuristics and Biases*. Cambridge, Mass.: Cambridge University Press.

Smith, J.Q. (1981) Search effort and the detection of faults. *British Journal of Mathematical and Statistical Psychology*, **34**, 181–193.

Snyder, G.H. (1972) Crisis bargaining. In: Hermann, C.F. (ed.)

International Crises: Insights from Behavioural Research. New York: The Free Press.

Solantous, T., Kimpela, M. and Taipale, V. (1984) The threat of war in the minds of 12-18-year-olds in Finland. *Lancet*, **8380**, 784-785.

Sonntag, P. (1981) *Verhinderung und Linderung atomarer Katastrophen.* Bonn: Osang.

Stockholm International Peace Research Institute (1977) *Yearbook. World Armaments and Disarmament.* London: Taylor and Francis.

Stockholm International Peace Research Institute (1981) *Yearbook. World Armaments and Disarmament.* London: Taylor and Francis.

Stockholm International Peace Research Institute (1982) *Yearbook. World Armaments and Disarmament.* London: Taylor and Francis.

Stockholm International Peace Research Institute (1983) *Yearbook. World Armaments and Disarmament.* London: Taylor and Francis.

Stockholm International Peace Research Institute (1984) *Yearbook. World Armaments and Disarmament.* London: Taylor and Francis.

Swank, R. (1949) Combat exhaustion. *Journal of Nervous and Mental Disorders*, **109**, 475.

Taylor, D.A., Wheeler, L. and Altman, I. (1968) Stress relations in socially isolated groups. *Journal of Personality and Social Psychology*, **9**, 369-376.

Thompson, J.A. (1983) *Non-cognitive factors in performance under stress.* Proceedings of a workshop on 'Stress effects - performance testing', held at the Institute of Naval Medicine, Gosport, 4 and 5 July 1983. Published by the Medical Research Council, PS 3/83.

Tichener, J.L. and Kapp, F.T. (1976) Family and character change at Buffalo Creek. *American Journal of Psychiatry*, **133**, 3, 295.

Time (1983) Behind closed doors. **No. 49**, 5 December, 12-23.

Times, The (1984) Quarter of Europe's US troops on drugs. **21 March.**

Titmuss, R.M. (1950) *Problems of Social Policy.* London: Longmans.

Tizard, B. (in press) The impact of the nuclear threat on child development: Problematic issues. *Harvard Educational Review.*

Tuchman, B. (1978) *A Distant Mirror.* New York: Knopf.

Turco, R.P., Toon, O.B., Ackerman, T.P., Pollack, J.B. and Sagan, C. (1983) Nuclear winter: Global consequences of multiple nuclear explosions. *Science*, **222**, 1283-1292.

Tversky, A. and Kahneman, D. (1971) The belief in the 'law of small numbers'. *Psychological Bulletin*, **76**, 105-110.

Tversky, A. and Kahneman, D. (1974) Judgement under uncertainty: Heuristics and biases. *Science*, **185**, 1124-1131.

Tynehurst, J.S. (1951) Individual reactions to community disaster. *American Journal of Psychiatry*, **107**, 764.

Tysoe, M. (1982) Bargaining and negotiation. In: Colman, A. (ed.) *Cooperation and Competition in Humans and Animals*. New York: Van Nostrand Reinhold.

Ury, W. (1984) Personal communication.

Ury, W. and Smoke, R. (1984) *Beyond the hotline: Controlling a nuclear crisis*. A report to the United States Arms Control and Disarmament Agency. Nuclear Negotiation Project, Harvard Law School.

US Atomic Energy Commission and Department of Defence (1962) Cited in *Defence Monitor* (1981) Washington DC: Centre for Defense Information.

Van der Plight, J. and Eiser, J.R. (in press) Nuclear energy: beliefs, values and acceptability. Presented at the Annual Meeting of the British Association for the Advancement of Science. *Interdisciplinary Science Reviews*.

Wallace, A.F. (1956) *Tornado in Worcester*. National Academy of Sciences Disaster Study No. 3. Washington DC: National Academy of Sciences.

Wallace, M.C. (1981) Old nails in new coffins: the para bellum hypothesis revisited. *Journal of Peace Research*, **18**(1), 91–95.

Wason, P. (1960) On the failure to eliminate hypotheses in a conceptual task. *Quarterly Journal of Experimental Psychology*, **12**, 129–140.

Watkins, J. (1970) In: Borger, R. and Cioffi, F. (eds) *Explanation in the Social Sciences*. Cambridge: Cambridge University Press.

Weisenbaum, J. (1983) Personal communication.

Wilkenfeld, J. and Brecher, M. (1982) Superpower crises management behaviour. In: Kegley, C.W. and McGowan, P. (eds) *Sage International Yearbook of Foreign Policy Studies*. Beverley Hills: Sage.

Wolfenstein, M. (1957) *Disaster: a Psychological Essay*. London: Routledge and Kegan Paul.

Wye, T. (pseud.) (1971) Will they fire in the hole? *Family* (supplement of the Air Force Magazine), **17 Nov.**

INDEX